S0-AEP-885

Study Guide

for Siegel's

Criminology
The Core

HV
6025
.S48
2007
Suppl.

Study Guide

for Siegel's

Criminology
The Core

Lynn Newhart
Rockford College

WADSWORTH
———————✦———————
THOMSON LEARNING

Australia • Canada • Mexico • Singapore • Spain • United Kingdom • United States

KWOO WITHDRAWN
KALAMAZOO VALLEY
COMMUNITY COLLEGE
LIBRARY

COPYRIGHT © 2002 Wadsworth Group. Wadsworth, is an imprint of the Wadsworth Group, a division of Thomson Learning, Inc. Thomson Learning™ is a trademark used herein under license.

ALL RIGHTS RESERVED. No part of this work covered by the copyright hereon may be reproduced or used in any form or by any means—graphic, electronic, or mechanical, including photocopying, recording, taping, Web distribution, or information storage and retrieval systems—without the prior written permission of the publisher.

Printed in Canada
1 2 3 4 5 6 7 04 03 02 01 00

For permission to use material from this text, contact us by **Web**: http://www.thomsonrights.com **Fax:** 1-800-730-2215 **Phone:** 1-800-730-2214

For more information, contact
Wadsworth/Thomson Learning
10 Davis Drive
Belmont, CA 94002-3098
USA

For more information about our products, contact us:
Thomson Learning Academic Resource Center
1-800-423-0563
http://www.wadsworth.com

International Headquarters
Thomson Learning
International Division
290 Harbor Drive, 2nd Floor
Stamford, CT 06902-7477
USA

UK/Europe/Middle East/South Africa
Thomson Learning
Berkshire House
168-173 High Holborn
London WC1V 7AA
United Kingdom

Asia
Thomson Learning
60 Albert Complex, #15-01
Singapore 189969

Canada
Nelson Thomson Learning
1120 Birchmount Road
Toronto, Ontario M1K 5G4
Canada

ISBN 0-534-51943-1

Table of Contents

Preface

Preface

This study guide is designed for use in conjunction with *Criminology: The Core, First Edition*, by Larry Siegel. It has two main purposes: (1) to provide you with an overview of the material found in the textbook; and (2) to provide you with study questions that will help you review for exams.

Each chapter begins with a list of learning objectives that you should be able to accomplish upon reading the chapter. A list of keywords follows the learning objectives, and a detailed chapter outline is provided, offering you a thorough overview of key points from the chapter.

Following each chapter outline, I have included 20 multiple choice statements, 15 true/false statements, 15 fill-in review questions, and 5 essay questions. An answer key containing answers to all questions but the essays can be found at the end of each chapter.

I would suggest that you treat the questions in each of these chapters as if they were actual exam questions. Once you have completed each section, check your answers and see if you have "passed." I hope that you find these review questions helpful, and hope you find studying criminology as exciting as I do. Good luck!

This manual, as with any project, involved the work of several people. I would like to thank Dawn Mesa of Wadsworth for her encouragement and guidance, Sue Smith and Tori Caprio for their formatting and proof-reading, and last, but not least, my daughter, Megan Glann. Meg served as my research assistant on this project and devoted many hours to searching the Internet for suitable sites, and reviewing videos that would be appropriate.

Your comments and questions are welcome. Please address them to Lynn Newhart, Coordinator, Criminal Justice Program, Rockford College, 5050 East State Street, Rockford, IL 61108-2393. Email: drnewhart@hotmail.com

1   *Crime and Criminology*

LEARNING OBJECTIVES

After covering the material in this chapter, you should understand:

1. the impact of Beccaria's work on contemporary criminology.

2. the basic tenets of positivism.

3. the influence of Emile Durkheim on contemporary criminology.

4. the different viewpoints of crime held by the following criminological perspectives: classical/choice, biological/psychological, structural process, conflict, and integrated.

5. the primary focus of the various subareas of the field of criminology.

6. how the consensus, conflict, and interactionist views of crime contrast and compare.

7. how the concept of criminal law was developed drawing on the Code of Hammurabi, the Mosaic Code, and English Common Law.

8. that the government expects to achieve a variety of social goals by outlawing certain behaviors.

9. the elements required for an act to be considered a crime.

10. why various research methods are used by criminologists.

11. that ethical issues are of great concern to criminologists.

KEYWORDS

anomie
Chicago School
socialization
conflict theory
rational choice theory
social structure
valid
reliable
white-collar crime
penology
rehabilitation
capital punishment
mandatory sentences
victimology
deviance
crime
consensus view
criminal law
conflict view
interactionist view
Code of Hammurabi

Mosaic Code
precedent
common law
statutory crimes
felony
misdemeanor
actus reus
mens rea
strict liability crimes
excuse defense
justification defense
appellate court
sampling
population
cross-sectional research
longitudinal research
cohort
Uniform Crime Report (UCR)
experimental research

CHAPTER OUTLINE

I.   A brief history of criminology
            1.   influence of Cesare Beccaria
            2.   classical criminology consists of four basic elements:
                  a.   people have free will to choose solutions
                  b.   criminal solutions may appear more attractive
                  c.   choice of criminal solutions may be controlled by fear of punishment
                  d.   punishment should be severe, certain, and swift

A.   Positivism
            1.   Auguste Comte - founder of sociology
            2.   positivism has two main elements:
                  a.   human behavior is a function of external forces that are often beyond individual control
                  b.   reliance on the scientific method
             3.   Cesare Lomboro is known as the "father of criminology"
                  a.   argued there are "born criminals"
                        1.   atavistic anomalies
            4.   strict biological determinism is no longer taken seriously

B.   Sociological criminology
            1.   traced the works of L.A.J. (Adolphe) Quetelet, and Emile Durkheim
            2.   Quetelet used social statistics to investigate the influence of social factors on the propensity to commit crime
            3.   Durkheim argued that crime is normal
            4.   Chicago School sociologists pioneered research on the social ecology
            5.   1930s and 1940s another group of sociologists began conducting research that linked the quality of an individual's socialization to criminal behavior

C.   Conflict criminology
            1.   Karl Marx's writings during the nineteenth century laid the foundations for what was to become Marxist criminology in the 1960s
            2.   the Marxist tradition indicts the economic system for producing the conditions that support a high crime rate

D. Contemporary criminology
   1. the various schools of criminology have evolved over the past 200 years
      a. classical theory has evolved into modern rational choice theory
      b. Lombrosian theory has evolved into contemporary biosocial and psychological views
      c. Chicago School has been updated in social structure theories
   2. modern rational choice theory argues that criminals are rational decision makers
      a. use available information to choose criminal or conventional behaviors
      b. their choice is structured by the fear of punishment
   3. biological and psychological theorists study the association between criminal behavior and such traits as diet, hormonal makeup, personality, and intelligence
   4. social structure theories maintain that social ecology directly controls criminal behavior
   5. some modern theorists believe that children learn to commit crime by interacting with and modeling their behavior after others they admire

II. What criminologists do: the criminological enterprise
   A. Criminal statistics
      1. involves measuring the amount and trends of criminal activity
      2. criminologists interested in criminal statistics try to create valid and reliable measurements of criminal behavior
      3. study of criminal statistics is one of the most crucial aspects of the criminological enterprise
         a. without valid and reliable data sources, efforts to conduct research on crime and create criminological theories would be futile
   B. Sociology of law
      1. a subarea of criminology concerned with the role social forces play in shaping criminal law and the role of criminal law in shaping society
      2. criminologists study the history of legal thought in an effort to understand how criminal acts evolved into their present form
      3. criminologists also actively participate in updating the content of criminal law
   C. Developing theories of crime causation
      1. some criminologists view crime as a function of personality, development, social learning or cognition
      2. others investigate the biological correlates of antisocial behavior and they study the biochemical, genetic, and neurological linkages to crime
      4. sociologists look at the social forces producing criminal behavior
   D. Understanding and describing criminal behavior
      1. involves research on specific criminal types and patterns
      2. Marvin Wolfgang's is considered a landmark analysis of the nature of homicide and the relationship between victim and offender
      3. Edwin Sutherland's analysis of business-related offenses (white-collar crime) described economic crime activities of the affluent.
   E. Penology
      1. involves the correction and control of known criminal offenders
         a. is the area of criminology which is most similar to the field of criminal justice
      2. some criminologists are advocates of rehabilitation and treatment
      3. others argue that crime can be controlled only through strict social control
      4. still others help to evaluate correctional initiatives to determine if they are effective and how they impact people's lives

F.   Victimology
1. criminologists recognize the critical role of the victim in the criminal justice process
    a. the victim's behavior is often a key determinant of crime
2. victimologists are particularly interested in victim surveys, victimization risk, victim culpability, and victim services

III.   Deviant or criminal: how criminologists define crime
A.   How is deviance defined?
1. three most common concepts of crime:
    a. consensus
    b. conflict
    c. interactionist
2. consensus view of crime argues that law defines crime
    a. there is agreement on outlawed behavior
    b. that laws apply equally to all citizens
3. conflict view of crime argues that the law is a tool of the ruling class
    a. crime is a politically defined concept
    b. "real crimes" are not outlawed
    c. the law is used to control the underclass
4. interactionist perspective of crime argues that moral entrepreneurs define crime
    a. crimes are illegal because society defines them that way
    b. criminal labels are life transforming events

IV.   Crime and the criminal law
1. most famous set of written laws of the ancient world is known as the Code of Hammurabi
2. the Mosaic Code, which is the foundation of Judeo-Christian moral teachings
    a. also a basis for the U.S. legal system
A.   Common law
1. royal judge used local custom and rules of conduct as his guide to a system known as *stare decisis*
2. courts were bound to follow the law established in previous cases unless a higher authority, such as the king or the pope, overruled the law
B.   Contemporary criminal law
1. acts prohibited by the criminal law constitute behaviors which those in power (i.e., the government) find unacceptable and unallowable
2. by outlawing certain behaviors, the government expects to achieve a variety of social goals:
    a. enforcing social control
    b. discouraging revenge
    c. expressing public opinion and morality
    d. deterring criminal behavior
    e. punishing wrongdoing
    f. maintaining social order
3. those who hold political power rely on criminal law to formally prohibit behaviors believed to either threaten societal well-being or challenge their authority
4. the law shifts the burden of revenge from the individual to the state
5. criminal law reflects constantly changing public opinions and moral values
6. criminal law has a social control function
    a. it can control, restrain, and direct human behavior through its sanctioning power
7. the deterrent power of criminal law is tied to the authority it gives the state to sanction or punish offenders
8. all legal systems are designed to support and maintain the boundaries of the social system they serve
C.   What are the elements of a crime?

1. prosecutor must show that the accused engaged in the guilty act (*actus reus*), and had criminal intent (*mens rea*) to commit the act
2. to satisfy the requirements of *actus reus,* guilty actions must be voluntary
   a. there are some instances when omission to act is considered criminal
3. in most situations, for an act to constitute a crime, it must be done with criminal intent
4. several crimes defined by statute do not require *mens rea*
   a. breaking a traffic law is an example

  D. Criminal defenses
1. a number of different approaches may be taken
2. defendants may deny *actus reus,* arguing that they were falsely accused
   a. they may argue that they lacked intent
3. justification -- the accused admits committing the criminal act, but maintains that the act was justified
4. "battered woman's defense"

  E. The evolution of criminal law
1. criminal law is constantly evolving in an effort to reflect social and economic conditions.
2. legal changes are prompted by highly publicized cases
3. future direction of U.S. criminal law remains unclear

V.   Criminological research methods

  A. Survey research
1. can measure the attitudes, beliefs, values, personality traits, and behavior of participants
   a. great deal of crime measurement is based on analysis of survey data, which is gathered using self-report surveys and interviews
2. characteristics of people or events in a carefully selected sample should be quite similar to those of the population at large
3. statistical analysis of data gathered from carefully drawn samples enables researchers to generalize their findings from small groups to large populations

  B. Cohort research
1. longitudinal research involves observing a group of people who share a like characteristic (cohort) over time

  C. Record data
1. aggregate data can tell us about the effect of social trends and patterns on the crime rate.
2. record data can be used to focus on the social forces that affect crime

  D. Experimental research
1. true experiments usually have three elements:
   a. random selections of subjects
   b. a control group
   c. an experimental condition

  E. Observational and interview research
1. sometimes criminologists focus their research on only a few subjects
2. bring participants into a structured laboratory setting and observing how they react to a predetermined condition or stimulus

VI.   Ethical Issues in Criminology
1. criminologists need to recognize the field's political and social consequences
2. must be both aware of the ethics of their profession and prepared to defend their work in the light of public scrutiny
3. must also be concerned about the subjects they study

VII.   Summary

MULTIPLE CHOICE

1. Beccaria believed in the concept of
    a. capital punishment.
    b. positivism.
    c. utilitarianism.
    d. torture.

2. During the nineteenth century, a new vision of the world challenged the validity of classical theory and presented an innovative way of looking at the causes of crime. This new vision was referred to as
    a. the interactionist perspective.
    b. positivism.
    c. conflict criminology.
    d. anomie.

3. Cesare Lombroso is known as the "father of _____."
    a. positivism
    b. classical criminology
    c. criminology
    d. utilitarianism

4. The foundations of sociological criminology can be traced to the work of Quetelet and _____
    a. Durkheim.
    b. Beccaria.
    c. Lombroso.
    d. Guerry.

5. The Chicago School sociologists examined how _____ influenced crime rates.
    a. gender
    b. age
    c. religion
    d. neighborhood conditions

6. Rational choice theory evolved from
    a. Lombrosian theory.
    b. social structure theory.
    c. classical theory.
    d. conflict theory.

7. The study of penology involves the correction and _____ of known criminal offenders.
    a. control
    b. incarceration
    c. rehabilitation
    d. punishment

8. The written code that defines crimes and their punishments is referred to as the
    a. Constitution.
    b. Bill of Rights.
    c. criminal law.
    d. statutory law.

9. According to the conflict view, the definition of crime is controlled by all but which of the following?
    a. wealth
    b. position

     c. power

     d. moral consensus

10. "Deviant behavior is behavior that people so label," reflects the _____ view of crime.
     a. interactionist
     b. consensus
     c. conflict
     d. deviance

11. The most famous set of written laws of the ancient world is known today as
     a. the Mosaic Code.
     b. the Code of Hammurabi.
     c. the Lombrosian Code.
     d. the criminal law.

12. Which of the following is not an example of a common-law crime?
     a. murder
     b. burglary
     c. arson
     d. substance abuse

13. Which of the following is an example of a *mala prohibitum* crime?
     a. murder
     b. burglary
     c. arson
     d. substance abuse

14. Which of the following crimes is not a felony?
     a. unarmed assault and battery
     b. murder
     c. rape
     d. burglary

15. Taking someone's money is an example of
     a. *actus reus.*
     b. *mens rea.*
     c. *actus mens.*
     d. *reus mens.*

16. Public welfare offenses are examples of
     a. common law violations.
     b. strict liability crimes.
     c. *mala in se* crimes.
     d. None of the above.

17. Insanity is a type of _____ defense.
     a. justification
     b. exotic.
     c. excuse
     d. invalid

18. The American legal system is a direct descendant of
     a. the Code of Hammurabi.
     b. the Mosaic Code.
     c. the British common law.
     d. the Greek common law.

19. _____ research follows a group of people who share some characteristic.
    a. Experimental
    b. Cohort
    c. Aggregate
    d. Record

20. Criminologists believe in all but one of the following perspectives:
    a. consensus view
    b. interactionist view
    c. intellectual view
    d. conflict view

TRUE/FALSE

1. The concept of utilitarianism argues the in their behavior choices, people want to achieve pleasure and pain.

2. Classical criminologists relied on the scientific method.

3. Cesare Beccaria is known as the "father of criminology."

4. According to Emile Durkheim's view of social positivism, crime is normal.

5. Chicago School sociologists argued that crime was a reaction to an environment that was inadequate for proper human relations and development.

6. The socialization view of crime was developed at the Chicago School.

7. The original Chicago School vision has been updated in the interactionist perspective.

8. The study of penology involves the rehabilitation of known criminal offenders.

9. According to the consensus view, crimes are behaviors that all elements of society consider to be repugnant.

10. According to the consensus view, crime is a political concept designed to protect the power and position of the upper classes at the expense of the poor.

11. Crimes defined by Parliament were referred to as statutory crimes.

12. *Mala prohibitum* crimes are almost universally prohibited.

13. Necessity is an example of an excuse defense.

14. The most important government database used by criminologists is the UCR.

15. Criminologists use very few research methods.

FILL-IN REVIEW

1. Criminology is an _____ science.

2. The more severe, certain, and _____ the punishment, the better able it is to control criminal behavior.

3. _____ see human behavior as a function of external forces that are often beyond individual control.

4. _____ version of strict biological determinism is no longer taken seriously.

5. The original Chicago School version has been updated in _____ theory.

6. Classical theory has evolved into modern _____ theory.

7. Criminologists interested in criminal statistics try to create _____ and _____ measurements of criminal behavior.

8. The subarea of criminology concerned with the role social forces play in shaping criminal law is known as the _____.

9. Edwin Sutherland's analysis of business-related offenses helped coin a new phrase, _____.

10. Criminologists view _____ as any action that departs from the social norms of society.

11. The term _____ implies general agreement among a majority of citizens on what behaviors should be prohibited by criminal law and hence viewed as crimes.

12. According to the _____ view, the definition of crime reflects preferences and opinions of people who hold social power in a particular legal jurisdiction.

13. Interactionists see criminal law as conforming to the beliefs of "_____."

14. The _____ is not only the foundation of Judeo-Christian moral teachings, but also a basis for the U.S. legal system.

15. "Battered woman's defense" is an example of a/an _____ defense.

ESSAY QUESTIONS

1. Typically, the law does not require people to aid people in distress. However, failure to act is considered a crime in certain instances. Discuss these instances.

2. Discuss the basic differences between the conflict and consensus views of crime.

3. By outlawing certain behaviors, the government expects to achieve a number of social goals. Discuss three of these goals.

4. Discuss the interactionist view of crime. How is it similar to the conflict view of crime?

5. Several susbareas exist within the broader arena of criminology. Select one of the sub-areas discussed in your text, and discuss it.

CHAPTER 1 ANSWER SECTION

MULTIPLE CHOICE

1. c
2. b
3. c
4. a
5. d
6. c
7. a
8. c
9. d
10. a
11. b
12. d
13. d
14. a
15. a
16. b
17. c
18. c
19. b
20. c

TRUE/FALSE

1. T
2. F
3. F
4. T
5. T
6. T
7. F
8. F
9. T
10. F
11. T
12. F
13. F
14. T
15. F

FILL-IN REVIEW

1. interdisciplinary
2. swift
3. Positivists
4. Lombroso's
5. social structure
6. rational choice
7. valid, reliable
8. sociology of law
9. white-collar crime
10. deviant behavior
11. consensus
12. interactionist
13. moral crusaders
14. Mosaic Code
15. exotic

2 *The Nature and Extent of Crime*

LEARNING OBJECTIVES

After covering the material in this chapter, you should understand:

1. the strengths and weaknesses of the Uniform Crime Report (UCR).

2. the strengths and weakness of the National Crime Victimization Survey (NCVS).

3. the differences between the UCR and NCVS.

4. concerns about self-report data.

5. the current violent crime and property crime trends.

6. the importance of crime patterns, as well as the impact of demographics on crime.

7. the meaning of the chronic offender concept.

KEYWORDS

Uniform Crime Report (UCR)
index crimes
National Crime Victimization Survey (NCVS)
self-report surveys
Brady law
instrumental crimes
expressive crimes
aging out (desistance)
masculinity hypothesis
chronic offenders

CHAPTER OUTLINE

I.   The Uniform Crime Report
       1.   best-known and most widely cited source of aggregate criminal statistics
       2.   FBI tallies and annually publishes the number of reported offenses by city, county, standard metropolitan area, and geographical division of the United States
       3.   shows the number and characteristics of individuals who have been arrested for the index crimes and all other crimes, expect traffic violations
       4.   uses three methods to express crime data:
           a.   the number of crimes reported to the police and arrests made are expressed as raw figures
           b.   crime rates per 100,000 people are computed
           c.   changes in the number and rate of crime over time are computed
       5.   accuracy is somewhat suspect
       6.   methodological issues also contribute to questions regarding the validity of the UCR

II.   Victim surveys
       1.   NCVS is the current method of assessing victimization in the United States

2. conducted by the U.S. Bureau of the Census in cooperation with the Bureau of Justice Statistics of the U.S. Department of Justice
3. relatively unbiased, valid estimate of all victimizations for the target crimes included in the survey

   A. NCVS findings
1. crime accounted for by the NCVS is considerably larger than the number of crimes reported to the FBI
2. if we are to believe the NCVS findings, the official UCR statistics do not provide an accurate picture of the crime problems because many crimes go unreported to the police

   B. Validity of the NCVS
1. may suffer some methodological problems:
     a. over- or underreporting of victimization
     b. inability to record the personal criminal activity of those interviewed
     c. sampling errors, and inadequate question format

III. Self-report surveys
1. ask people to reveal information about their own law violations
2. assumption is that assurance of anonymity and confidentiality encourages people to describe their illegal activities accurately
3. viewed as a mechanism to get at the "dark figures of crime"
4. most have focused on juvenile delinquency and youth crime
     a. also used to examine offense histories of prison inmate, drug user, and others
5. data obtained can be used to:
     a. test theories
     b. measure attitudes toward crime
     c. compute the association between crime and important social variables

   A. Self-report findings
1. indicate that the number of people who break the law is far greater than the number projected by official statistics
2. indicate that the most common offenses are truancy, alcohol abuse, use of a false ID, shoplifting or larceny under $50, fighting, marijuana use, and damage to the property of others
3. suggest that criminal activity is widespread and is not restricted to a few "bad apples"

   B. Accuracy of self-reports
1. methodological issues have been raised about the accuracy of self-reports:
     a. unreasonable to expect people to candidly admit illegal acts
     b. people may exaggerate their criminal acts or forget them
     c. comparisons between groups can be highly misleading
     d. "missing cases" phenomenon is of concern
     e. institutionalized youth are underrepresented

IV. Evaluating crime data
1. each source of crime data has its strengths and weaknesses
2. FBI survey is carefully tallied and contains information that other data sources lack,
     a. survey omits the many crime victims who choose not to report to the police
3. NCVS includes underreported crime and important information of personal characteristics of victims
     a. data consists of estimates made from relatively limited samples of the total U.S. population
     b. survey does not include data on important crime patterns, such as murder and drug abuse
4. self-reports surveys provide information on the personal characteristics of offenders
     a. these reports rely on the honesty of criminal offenders and drug abusers

5. despite their different tallies of crime, the crime patterns and trends they record are often quite similar

V. Crime trends
    1. In 1991, police recorded about 14.6 million crimes
        a. number of reported crimes has declined by about 3 million from the peak in 1991
    2. teen murder rate has also declined during the past few years
  A. Trends in violent crime
    1. violent crimes reported by the FBI include murder, rape, assault, and robbery
    2. according to the UCR, violence in the U.S. has decreased significantly during the past decade, reversing a long trend of skyrocketing increases
        a. decreases in the number and rate of murders have been particularly encouraging
    4. some cities, such as New York, report a decline of more than 50 percent in their murder rates through the 1990s
  B. Trends in property crime
    1. property crime reported in the UCR includes larceny, motor vehicle theft, and arson
    2. property crime rates have declined in recent years
        a. drop has not been as dramatic as that experienced by the violent crime rate
  C. Trends in self-reports and victimizations
    1. self-report results appear to be more stable than the UCR.
        a. uniform pattern emerges when surveys are compared over a 20-year period
    2. NCVS also shows that crime rates have undergone a major decline in the 1990s
  D. What the future holds
    1. Fox predicts a significant increase in teen violence if current trends persist
    2. Levitt disagrees
    3. is no way of telling what future changes may influence crime rates

VI. Crime patterns
  A. The ecology of crime
    1. most reported crimes occur during the warm summer months of July and August
        a. exceptions to this trend are murders and robberies
    2. crime rates may be higher on the first day of the month than at any other time
    3. crime rates increase with rising temperatures up to about 85 degrees, but then began to decline
        a. domestic assault continues to increase as the temperatures rise
    4. large urban areas have the highest violence rate; rural areas have the lowest per capita crime rates
  B. Use of firearms
    1. firearms play a dominant role in criminal activity
    2. Zimring and Hawkins believe that the proliferation of handguns and the high rate of lethal violence they cause is the single most significant factor separating the crime problem in the U.S. from the rest of the developed world
  C. Social class and crime
    1. traditionally crime has been thought of as a lower-class phenomenon
    2. selling narcotics is an example of instrumental crime
    3. rape and assault are examples of expressive crime
    4. official statistics indicate that victimization rates for both males and females in inner-city, high-poverty areas are generally higher than those in suburban or wealthier areas
    5. has been suggested that the relationship between official crime and social class is a function of law enforcement practices, not actual crime patterns
    6. police may devote more resources to poor areas, and they may be more likely to formally arrest and prosecute lower-class citizens

7. self-report data generally do not find a direct relationship between social class and youth crime
8. appears that the debate over the relationship between class and crime will most likely persist

D. Age and crime
 1. general agreement that age is inversely related to criminality
 2. young people are arrested at a disproportionate rate to their numbers in the population
 3. elderly are particularly resistant to the temptations of crime
 4. the fact that people commit less crime as they mature is referred to as aging out or desistance
 5. one view of aging out is that there is a direct relationship between aging and crime
 6. another view is that aging out is a function of the natural history of the human life cycle
 7. although most people age out of crime, some do pursue a criminal career

E. Gender and crime
 1. all three data-gathering criminal statistics tools support the theory that male crime rates are much higher than those of females
 2. masculinity hypothesis stated that few "masculine" females were responsible for the handful of crimes that women commit
 3. by the mid-twentieth century, criminologists commonly portrayed gender differences in the crime rate as a function of socialization
 4. in the 1970s, liberal feminists focused their attention on the social and economic role of women in society and their relationship to female crime rates
 5. female arrests rates seem to be increasing at a faster pace than male rates

F. Race and crime
 1. official data indicate that minority group members are involved in a disproportionate share of criminal activity
 2. nationwide self-report studies of youth have found few racial differences in crime rates
    a. black youths were much more likely to be arrested and taken into custody
 3. data seem to suggest that criminal behavior rates of black and white teenagers are generally similar
 4. recorded differences in the black and white violent crime arrest rates cannot be explained away solely by racism or differential treatment within the criminal justice system
 5. most explanations of racial patterns and crime focus on:
    a. impact of economic deprivation
    b. social disorganization
    c. subcultural adaptations
    d. the legacy of racism and discrimination on personality and behavior

VII. The chronic offender
 1. most offenders commit a single criminal act, and upon arrest, discontinue their antisocial activity
 2. small group of persistent offenders accounts for a majority of all criminal offenses
 3. concept of the chronic offender is most closely associated with the research efforts of Wolfgang, Figlio, and Sellin in the 1970s
 4. Wolfgang and his associates found that arrests and court experience did little to deter the chronic offender
 5. findings of recent cohort studies and the discovery of the chronic offender have revitalized criminological theory
 6. traditional theories of criminal behavior have failed to distinguish between chronic and occasional offenders

VIII. Summary

MULTIPLE CHOICE

1. The Federal Bureau of Investigation's _____ is the best-known and most widely cited source of aggregate criminal statistics.
    a. National Crime Victimization Survey
    b. Federal Crime Survey
    c. Uniform Crime Report
    d. Federal Crime Report

2. In the UCR, crime rates are computed per _____ people.
    a. 1,000
    b. 10,000
    c. 100,000
    d. 100,000,000

3. The _____ is the current method of assessing victimization in the U.S.
    a. UCR
    b. NCVS
    c. FCR
    d. FCS

4. The number of crimes accounted for by the NCVS is _____ than the number of crimes reported to the FBI.
    a. considerably larger
    b. considerably smaller
    c. about the same
    d. There is no way to make a comparison.

5. Self-report studies indicate that the most common offenses are all but which of the following?
    a. alcohol abuse
    b. use of a false ID
    c. truancy
    d. shoplifting over $50

6. Self-report studies show that about _____ percent of high school seniors report stealing in the past 12 months.
    a. 20
    b. 30
    c. 40
    d. 50

7. Official data show that the teen murder rate has _____ during the past few years.
    a. increased
    b. decreased
    c. stabilized
    d. increased, but only slightly

8. The violent crimes reported by the FBI include all but which of the following crimes?
    a. murder
    b. rape
    c. burglary
    d. assault

9. Property crimes include all but which of the following?
    a. larceny
    b. motor vehicle theft

c. arson
d. They are all included.

10. Most reported crimes occur during the months of
    a. February and January
    b. March and April
    c. May and June
    d. July and August

11. In 1999, the UCR reported that _____ percent of all murders involved firearms.
    a. 40
    b. 50
    c. 60
    d. 70

12. Crimes such as rape and assault are referred to as _____ crimes.
    a. expressive
    b. instrumental
    c. repressive
    d. excessive

13. As a general rule, the peak age for property crime is believed to be _____.
    a. 15
    b. 16
    c. 17
    d. 18

14. Elderly females are predominately arrested for
    a. alcohol-related matters.
    b. substance abuse.
    c. larceny.
    d. domestic abuse.

15. Lombroso's theory of the gender differences in the crime rate is known as the
    a. gender differential hypothesis.
    b. masculinity hypothesis.
    c. gender trait hypothesis
    d. aggression hypothesis

16. By the mid-twentieth century, criminologists commonly portrayed gender differences in the crime rate as a function of
    a. socialization.
    b. personality.
    c. androgen levels.
    d. psychological differences.

17. The increase in arrests of teenage girls between 1990 and 1999 was _____ the increase in male teenage arrests.
    a. double
    b. triple
    c. five times
    d. seven times

18. The weight of the evidence shows that there is little difference in self-reported overall crime rates by
    a. religion
    b. gender

     c. age
     d. race

19. The concept of the chronic offender is most closely associated with the research efforts of
     a. Wolfgang, Figlio, and Sellin.
     b. Lombroso.
     c. Donohue III and Levitt.
     d. Fox

20. One of the most important findings in the crime statistics in the existence of the _____.
     a. juvenile delinquent.
     b. occasional offender.
     c. chronic offender.
     d. elderly offender.

TRUE /FALSE

1. The NCVS tallies and annually publishes the number of reported offenses by city, county, standard metropolitan area, and geographical division of the U.S.

2. The UCR uses four methods to express crime data.

3. No federal crimes are reported in the UCR.

4. The NCVS is conducted by the U.S. Bureau of the Census in cooperation with the Bureau of Justice Statistics.

5. Self-report studies are viewed as a mechanism to get at the "dark figures of crime."

6. In general, self-report surveys indicate that the number of people who break the law is about the same as the number projected by official statistics.

7. Although their tallies of crimes are certainly not in synch, the crime patterns and trends recorded by the sources of crime data discussed in your text are often quite similar.

8. The murder statistics are generally regarded as the most accurate aspect of the UCR.

9. Murders and robberies occur most frequently in December and January.

10. Domestic assault, like most other crimes, tends to decline after the temperature reaches about 85 degrees.

11. Traditionally crime has been thought to be a lower-class phenomenon.

12. There is a general agreement that age is inversely related to criminality.

13. By middle age all but the most chronic offenders terminate their criminal behavior.

14. In the 1970s, liberal feminists suggested that the traditionally lower crime rate for women could be explained by the "masculinity hypothesis."

15. Traditionally theories of criminal behavior have failed to distinguish between chronic and occasional offenders.

FILL-IN-REVIEW

1. There are _____ and _____ patterns in the crime rate.

2. Some criminologists suggest that _____, such as police profiling, accounts for the racial differences in the crime rate.

3. The _____ is an annual tally of crimes reported to local police department.

4. The _____ samples more than 50,000 people annually in order to estimate the total number of criminal incidents, including those not reported to the police.

5. Self-report surveys ask respondents about _____.

6. Crime is more common during the _____ and in _____ areas.

7. The true association between _____ and _____ is still unknown.

8. The female crime rate appears to be _____.

9. The number of crimes accounted for by the NCVS is _____ than the number of crimes reported to the FBI.

10. At least _____ of all U.S. high school students engaged in theft during the past year.

11. The violent crimes reported by the FBI include murder, rape, assault, and _____.

12. Property crimes reported in the UCR include motor vehicle theft, arson, and _____.

13. Those unable to obtain desired goods and service through conventional means may resort to theft and other illegal activities –such as selling narcotics to obtain them. These activities are referred to as _____.

14. More than 20 years ago, Title, Vilemez, and Smith concluded that little if any support exists for the contention that crime is primarily a _____.

15. There is general agreement that _____ is inversely related to criminality.

ESSAY QUESTIONS

1. All three data-gathering criminal statistics tools support the theory that male crime rate are much higher than those of females. Discuss what your text tells us about the gender differences in crime.

2. Discuss what your text tells about the relationship between race and crime. How can these racial patterns be explained?

3. The accuracy of the UCR is somewhat suspect. Discuss why this is so.

4. Several methodological issues have been raised about the accuracy of self-report data. Discuss these issues.

5. It is always risky to speculate about the future of crime trends, yet some criminologists have tried to predict future patterns. Discuss the predictions of criminologist James A. Fox. Why are his predictions persuasive?

Due Feb 1ˢ +
via meg

TRUE/FALSE

1.	F
2.	F
3.	T
4.	T
5.	T
6.	F
7.	T
8.	T
9.	T
10.	F
11.	T
12.	T
13.	F
14.	F
15.	T

10.	d
11.	d
12.	a
13.	b
14.	c
15.	b
16.	a
17.	b
18.	d
19.	a
20.	c

FILL-IN REVIEW

1. stable, enduring
2. institutional racism
3. FBI's Uniform Crime Report
4. National Crime Victimization Survey
5. their own criminal activity
6. summer, urban
7. class, crime
8. rising
9. considerably larger
10. one-third
11. robbery
12. larceny
13. instrumental crimes
14. lower-class phenomenon
15. age

3 Victims and Victimization

LEARNING OBJECTIVES

After covering the material in this chapter, you should understand:

1. problems suffered by crime victims: economic, long-term stress, and fear.

2. victimizations suffered because of the justice system.

3. the impact of victimization on future criminal behavior.

4. patterns of victimization.

5. the social ecology of victimization.

6. demographic information about victims.

7. relationships between victims and their offenders.

8. the various theoretical explanations of victimization.

9. the concepts of victim precipitation, active precipitation, and passive precipitation.

10. services offered to victims and their families.

11. victims' rights.

KEYWORDS

victimology
victimologists
posttraumatic stress disorder
cycle of violence
victim precipitation theory
active precipitation
passive precipitation
lifestyle theories
deviant place theory
routine activities theory
suitable targets
capable guardians
motivated offenders
victim-witness assistance program
compensation
crisis intervention
victim–offender reconciliation program
preventive detention
target hardening

CHAPTER OUTLINE

I.   Problems of crime victims
    A.   Economic loss
        1.   victims lose about $11 billion per year
        2.   crime produces social costs that must be paid by nonvictims as well
        3.   victims may suffer long-term losses in earnings and occupational attainment
    B.   System abuse
        1.   victims may suffer victimization by the justice system
        2.   victims may suffer economic hardship because of wages lost while they testify in court
    C.   Long-term stress
        1.   victims may suffer stress and anxiety long after the incident is over
        2.   children who are victimized are more likely to escape their environment
            a.   high risk for juvenile arrest/ involvement with the justice system
        3.   spousal abuse victims suffer high prevalence of depression, and various disorders
        4.   some victims are physically disabled as result of wounds sustained during episodes of random violence
    D.   Fear
        1.   victims remain fearful long after their wounds have healed
        2.   victims of violent crime are most deeply affected
            a.   more likely to suffer psychological stress for extended periods of time
    E.   Antisocial behavior
        1.   growing evidence that crime victims are more likely to commit crime themselves
        2.   this phenomenon is referred to as the cycle of violence

II.   The nature of victimization
        1.   patterns in victimization survey findings are stable and repetitive
    A.   The social ecology of victimization
        1.   NCVS shows that
            a.   crimes are slightly more likely to take place in an open, public area
            b.   more serious violent crimes typically take place after 6 P.M.
            c.   lesser forms of violence are more likely to occur during the daytime
        2.   neighborhood characteristics affect the chances of victimization
            a.   central city dwellers have significantly higher rates
            b.   risk of murder for both men and women is significantly higher in dis-organized inner-city areas
    B.   The victim's household
        1.   people who own their homes are less vulnerable than renters
        2.   recent population movement and changes may account for decreases in crime victimization
        3.   smaller households in less populated areas have a lower victimization risk
    C.   Victim characteristics
        1.   gender affects victimization risk
            a.   males are much more likely to be victims of violent crime, with the exception of rape and sexual assault
            b.   men are almost twice as likely as women to experience aggravated assault and robbery
            c.   women are seven times more likely to be victims of rape or sexual assault
        2.   young people face a much greater risk of victimization than do older persons
            a.   teens are 35 more times likely to be raped or sexually assaulted than people ages 50-64
            b.   people over 65 account for only 1 percent of violent victimizations
        3.   poorest Americans are most likely victims of violent crime
            a.   wealthy more likely targets of personal theft crimes
        4.   martial status influences victimization

         a.   never-married males and females are victimized more often than married
    5.   African Americans are more likely than European Americans to be victims of violent crime
         a.   three times more likely to be victims of robbery/twice as likely to experience aggravated assault
         b.   young black males face a murder risk eight times higher than that of young white males
    6.   Hispanics much more likely than non-Hispanics to fall victim to robbery and aggravated assault
    7.   households that have experienced victimization in the past are more likely to experience it in the future
    8.   three types of characteristics increase potential for victimization
         a.   target vulnerability
         b.   target gratifiability
         c.   target antagonism

  D.   The victims and their criminals
    1.   victims report most crimes were committed by a single offender over age 20
    2.   crimes tend to be intraracial
    3.   substance abuse was involved in about one-third of violent crime incidents
    4.   a surprising number of crimes are committed by relatives or acquaintances of the victim

III.   Theories of victimization
  A.   Victim precipitation theory
    1.   some people actually initiate the confrontation that leads to victimization
         a.   active precipitation occurs when victims act provocatively
         b.   passive precipitation occurs when the victim exhibits some personal characteristics that unknowingly threatens or encourages the attacker
  B.   Lifestyle theories
    1.   people may become crime victims because of their lifestyles
    2.   crime is not a random occurrence, but a function of victim's lifestyle
    3.   those who have high-risk lifestyle have a greater chance of victimization
         a.   runaways
         b.   teenage males
         c.   young adults
  C.   Deviant place theory
    1.   victims do not encourage crime/ they are victims because of where they reside
         a.   socially disorganized high-crime areas
  D.   Routine activities theory
    1.   assumes that both the motivation to commit crime and the supply of offenders are constant
    2.   interaction of three variables reflect routine activities of typical American lifestyle
         a.   availability of suitable targets
         b.   absence of capable guardians
         c.   presence of motivated offenders

IV.   Caring for the victim
    1.   almost every American age 12 and over will one day become the victim of a common-law crime
    2.   President Reagan created Task Force on Victims of Crime n 1982
    3.   Congress passed the Omnibus Victim and Witness Protection Act
         a.   use of victim impact statements
         b.   greater protection for witnesses
         c   stringent bail laws
         d.   use of restitution
    4.   the Comprehensive Crime Control Act and the Victims of Crime Act in 1984

A. Victim service programs
   1. estimated there are 2,000 victim-witness assistance programs in the U.S.
   2. primary goal of victim advocates has been to lobby for crime victim compensation
   3. court services include explanations of court procedures and transportation to and from court
   4. public education programs help familiarize the general public with victim advocate services
   5. more than half of all victim programs provide crisis intervention for victims
   6. victim-offender reconciliation programs use mediators to facilitate face-to-face encounters between victims and their attackers

B. Victims' rights
   1. Carrington suggests that crime victims have legal rights that should assure them basic services from the government
     a. rights range from adequade protection from violent crime to victim compensation and assistance from the criminal justice system

C. Self-protection
   1. concept of target hardening means making one's home and business crime-proof
   2. there is mounting evidence that people who protect their homes are less likely to be victimized

D. Community organization
   1. some communities have organized on the neighborhood level against crime
   2. there is little evidence that such programs reduce crime

V. Summary

MULTIPLE CHOICE

1. Each heroin addict is estimated to cost society more than _____ per year.
   a. $135,000
   b. $145,000
   c. $150,00
   d. $175,000

2. Girls who were psychologically, sexually, or physically abused as children were more likely to have lower-self-esteem and be more _____ as adults than those who were not abused.
   a. homicidal
   b. promiscuous
   c. suicidal
   d. All of the above.

3. The abuse-crime phenomenon is referred to as the _____
   a. cycle of abuse.
   b. cycle of abuse-crime.
   c. cycle of depressive tendencies.
   d. cycle of violence.

4. Patterns in the victimization survey findings are stable and repetitive, suggesting that victimization is not random but a function of personal and _____ factors.
   a. ecological
   b. biological
   c. social
   d. psychological

5. Less serious forms of violence, such as _____ and personal larcenies like purse snatching are more likely to take occur during the daytime.
   a. arson
   b. burglary
   c. unarmed robbery
   d. motor vehicle theft

6. Rural areas have a victimization rate almost _____ that of city dwellers.
   a. one-third
   b. double
   c. one-half
   d. three-fourths

7. Poor, rural European homes in the _____ are least likely to contain crime victims or be the target of theft offenses.
   a. southeast
   b. southwest
   c. northwest
   d. northeast

8. For all crimes, males are _____ percent more likely to be victimized than females.
   a. 15
   b. 22
   c. 33
   d. 50

9. Teens are _____ more likely to be raped or sexually assaulted than people ages 50 – 64.
   a. 25

b. 35

c. 45

d. 55

10. African Americans are _____ time more likely to be the victims of robbery than European Americans.
    a. two
    b. three
    c. four
    d. five

11. Three specific types of characteristics have been found to increase the potential for victimization. Which of the following is not one of these types?
    a. target vulnerability
    b. target gratifiability
    c. target antagonism
    d. target hostility

12. _____ precipitation occurs when victims act provocatively, use threats, or fighting words, or even attack first.
    a. Active
    b. Passive
    c. Reactive
    d. Proactive

13. _____ precipitation may occur when the victim belongs to a group whose mere presence threatens the attacker's reputation, status, or economic well-being.
    a. Active
    b. Passive
    c. Reactive
    d. Proactive

14. _____ theory was first articulated in a series of papers by Cohen and Felson.
    a. Deviant place
    b. Lifestyle
    c. Routine activities
    d. Victim precipitation

15. Both routine activities theories and the lifestyle approach rely on four basic concepts. Which of the following is not one of these concepts?
    a. proximity to criminals
    b. guardianship
    c. target hostility
    d. time of exposure to criminals

16. Surveys show that upward of _____ percent of the general public has been victimized by crime at least once in their lives.
    a. 25
    b. 33
    c. 50
    d. 75

17. Reconciliation programs are based on the concept of _____.
    a. rehabilitation.
    b. restorative justice.
    c. punitive correctional measures.
    d. treatment.

18. Victims are not entitled to be present at parole hearings in _____ states.
    a. 20
    b. 22
    c. 36
    d. 37

19. Making one's home and business crime-proof through the use of locks, bars, and other devices is known as
    a. target deterring.
    b. target denying.
    c. target hardening.
    d. target fortifying.

20. Surveys suggest that about _____ of all students are injured in a physical altercation each year in school buildings.
    a. one-fourth
    b. one-third
    c. one-half
    d. two-thirds

TRUE/FALSE

1. There is growing evidence that people who are crime victims also seem more likely to commit crime themselves.

2. Victim data reveal that victim risk diminishes rapidly after age 25.

3. The wealthy are more likely to be targets of burglary and robbery than are the poor.

4. Victim data tell us that most crimes were committed by two or more offenders.

5. According to the lifestyle theory, some people may actually initiate the confrontation that eventually leads to their injury or death.

6. National victim surveys indicate that almost every American age 12 and over will one day become the victim of common-law crimes.

7. Results of victimization surveys suggest that victimization is random.

8. Victimization surveys indicate that neighborhood characteristics affect the chances of victimization.

9. Recent population movement and changes may account for recent decreases in crime victimization.

10. The most important factors to distinguish victims and nonvictims are gender, age, race, and religion.

11. The poorest Americans are also the most likely victims of violent crime.

12. Crimes tend to be interracial.

13. Cohen and Felson assume that both the motivation to commit crime and the supply of targets are constant.

14. Cohen and Felson argue that crime rates increased between 1960 and 1980 as a result of increased female participation in the workforce.

15. One of the primary goals of victim advocates has been to lobby for legislation creating crime victim compensation programs.

FILL-IN REVIEW

1. _____ is the branch of criminology that examines the nature and extent of crime victimization.

2. Victims suffer long-term trauma, including _____ _____ disorder.

3. The association between _____ and _____ is undoubtedly tied to lifestyle.

4. Women are more likely than men to be attacked by a _____.

5. The wealthy are more likely to be the targets of _____ _____.

6. _____ _____ theory suggests that crime victims may trigger attacks by acting aggressively or provocatively.

7. Some experts link victimization to _____ _____, which include going out late at night and living in dangerous neighborhoods.

8. The _____ _____ approach suggests that the risk of victimization can be understood as an interaction among suitable targets, effective guardians, and motivated criminals.

9. An estimated 2,000 _____ _____ programs have been developed throughout the U.S.

10. A common victim program service helps victims deal with the criminal justice system. One approach is to prepare victims and witnesses by explaining _____ _____.

11. More than half of all victim programs provide _____ _____ for victims who feel isolated, vulnerable, and in need of immediate services.

12. _____ _____ programs use mediators to facilitate face-to-face encounter between victims and their attackers.

13. Leal scholar Carrington suggests that victims should be allowed to participate in _____.

14. About 14 states have within their legal codes a _____ _____ _____ _____.

15. The concept of _____ _____ refers to making one's home and business crime-proof through the use of locks, bars, alarms, and other devices.

ESSAY QUESTIONS

1. There is growing evidence that crime victims are more likely to commit crime themselves. Discuss what the research tells us about this evidence.

2. Discuss the social ecology of victimization in terms of the victim's household and age.

3. Finkelhor and Asigian have found that three specific types of characteristics increase the potential for victimization. Discuss each of these.

4. Discuss the deviant place theory. Do you agree with the basic assumptions of this theory? Why or why not?

5. Helping the victim of crime to cope is the responsibility of all of society. Discuss three of the victim service programs that were discussed in your text.

CHAPTER 3 ANSWER SECTION

MULTIPLE CHOICE

1.	a
2.	c
3.	d
4.	a
5.	c
6.	c
7.	d
8.	b
9.	b
10.	b
11.	d
12.	a
13.	b
14.	c
15.	c
16.	d
17.	b
18.	c
19.	c
20.	b

TRUE/FALSE

1.	T
2.	T
3.	F
4.	F
5.	F
6.	T
7.	F
8.	T
9.	T
10.	F
11.	T
12.	F
13.	F
14.	T
15.	T

FILL-IN REVIEW

1. Victimology
2. posttraumatic stress
3. age, victimization
4. relative
5. personal theft
6. Victim precipitation
7. high-risk lifestyles
8. routine activities
9. victim-witness assistance
10. court procedures
11. crisis intervention
12. Victim-offender reconciliation
13. sentencing
14. Victims' Bill of Rights
15. target hardening

4   *Choice Theory: Because They Want to*

LEARNING OBJECTIVES

After covering the material in this chapter, you should understand:

1. the main concepts of rational choice theory.

2. why choice theorists view crime as both offense- and offender-specific.

3. what personal factors condition people to choose criminality.

4. how the decision to commit crime is structured.

5. how and why criminals learn techniques of crime.

6. explanations of the rationality of crime.

7. the seductions of crime.

8. ways of preventing crime.

9. consequences of situational crime prevention efforts.

10. the concept of general deterrence.

11. why capital punishment fails.

12. assumptions of the specific deterrence theory.

13. the concepts of stigmatization and reintegrative shaming.

14. the logic behind incarceration.

15. what the three strikes and you're out policy means.

KEYWORDS

rational choice
choice theory
classical criminology
offense-specific
offender-specific
edgework
seductions of crime
situational crime prevention
defensible space
displacement
extinction
diffusion of benefits
discouragement
general deterrence
crackdown

brutalization effect
informal sanctions
specific deterrence
incarceration
recidivism
probation
stigmatization
reintegrative shaming
incapacitation effect
three strikes and you're out
just desert

CHAPTER OUTLINE

I.   The development of rational choice theory
        1. has its roots in the classical school of criminology developed by Beccaria
        2. classical criminology remained popular until middle of twentieth century

II.   The concepts of rational choice
        1. law-violating behavior is the product of careful thought and planning
        2. offenders consider personal needs and situational factors
        A. Offense and offender specifications
            1. crime is viewed as both offense- and offender-specific
            2. crime is an event; criminality is a personal trait
            3. criminals do not commit crime all the time
        B. Structuring criminality
            1. personal factors condition people to choose criminality
            2. learning and experience may be important elements in structuring
                criminality
            3. personality and lifestyle affect criminal choices
        C. Structuring crime
            1. decision to commit crime is structured by:
                a. where it occurs
                b. the characteristics of the target
                c. available means

III.   Is crime rational?
        1. evidence exists that street crimes may be the product of calculated risk
        2. signs of rationality are evident in the choices made by armed robbers
        3. research shows that at its onset, drug use is controlled by rational decision-
            making
        4. drug dealers approach their profession in a businesslike fashion
        5. evidence confirms that violent criminals rationally select suitable targets

IV.   Why do people commit crime?
        1. crime is more attractive than law-abiding behavior
        2. according to Katz there are immediate benefits to criminality

V.   Situational crime prevention
        1. criminal acts will be avoided if:
            a. potential targets are guarded
            b. the means to commit crime are controlled
            c. potential offenders are monitored
        2. defensible space means that crime can be prevented or displaced through
            residential design
        A. Crime prevention strategies

               1.   crime prevention tactics fall into one of four categories:
                  a.   increase the effort needed to commit crime
                  b.   increase the risk of committing crime
                  c.   reduce the rewards for committing crime
                  d.   induce guilt or shame for committing crime

B.   Displacement, extinction, discouragement, and diffusion
               1.   situational crime prevention efforts may produce unforeseen and unwanted consequences
               2.   there may also be advantages
                  a.   diffusion of benefits can occur
                  b.   situational crime prevention may produce discouragement

VI.   General deterrence
               1.   motivated people will violate the law if left free and unrestricted
               2.   general deterrence argues that decision to commit crime can be controlled by threat of capital punishment

A.   Certainty of punishment
               1.   arrest rates should decline if certainty of arrest, conviction, and sanctioning increase
               2.   the relationship between certainty of punishment and crime rates is far from settled
               3.   certainty of punishment may be race-specific

B.   Level of police activity
               1.   there is not strong evidence to suggest that adding police leads to reduced crime rates
               2.   research shows that efforts such as crackdowns have not been successful in lowering crime rates
               3.   crime rates are reduced when police officers use aggressive problem-solving and community improvement techniques

C.   Severity of punishment
               1.   some studies show that increasing sanction levels can control common criminal behaviors
                  a.   little consensus that strict punishments alone reduce criminal activities

D.   Capital punishment
               1.   research on capital punishment as a deterrent can be divided into three types:
                  a.   immediate impact studies
                  b.   comparative research
                  c.   time-series analysis
               2.   a number of criminologists find that executions actually increase murder rates; others argue that their immediate impact is to lower murder rates
               3.   comparison of murder rates in jurisdictions that have abolished the death penalty with the rates in those that have not show that there is little difference
               4.   time-series analysis shows that capital punishment is no more effective as a deterrent than life imprisonment
               5.   the failure of the "ultimate deterrent" to deter the "ultimate crime" has been used by critics to question the validity of the hypothesis that severe punishment will lower crime rates

E.   Swiftness of punishment
               1.   general deterrence theory holds that people who believe they will be punished swiftly if they break the law will abstain from crime

F.   Informal sanctions
               1.   evidence is accumulating that fear of informal sanctions may in fact reduce crime

          2.   research shows that threat of informal sanctions can be a more effective
                deterrent than formal sanctions
     G.   Critiques of general deterrence
          1.   the relationship between crime rates and deterrent measures is far less than
                choice theorists might expect
          2.   neither the perception nor the reality of punishment can deter most crimes

VII.   Specific deterrence
          1.   holds that criminal sanctions should be so powerful that known criminals
                will never repeat their criminal acts
     A.   Does specific deterrence deter crime?
          1.   research on chronic offenders indicates arrest and punishment have little
                effect on experienced criminals
          2.   incarceration may slow down or delay recidivism in the short term
                a.   overall probability of rearrest does not change following
                      incarceration
                b.   offenders receiving community sentences have rates of recidivism
                      similar to those who are sentenced to prison
          3.   some research suggests that severe punishment increases reoffending rates
     B.   Stigmatization versus reintegrative shaming
          1.   Braithwaite helps explain why specific deterrence measures may fail
                a.   punishment stigmatizes offenders, sets them outside the
                      mainstream
                b.   offenders see themselves as victims of the justice system
          2.   concept of shame is divided into two distinct types:
                a.   stigmatization
                b.   reintegrative shaming

VIII.   Incapacitation
     A.   Can incapacitation reduce crime?
          1.   research on direct benefits of incapacitation has been inconclusive
     B.   The logic behind incapacitation
          1.   evaluations of incarceration strategies reveal that their impact is less than
                expected
          2.   little evidence that incarceration deters future criminality
          3.   economics suggest there will always be someone to take the place of the
                incarcerated offender
          4.   most criminal offenses are committed by teens and very young adult
                offenders
          5.   incapacitation strategy is very expensive, costs billions of dollars annually
     C.   Three strikes and you're out
          1.   people convicted of three felony offenses are given a mandatory life
                sentence
          2.   this may not work for several reasons:
                a.   most convicted for three strikes are aging out of crime
                b.   current sentences for violent crime are quite severe now
                c.   larger prison populations will increase already high prison costs
                d.   there would be racial disparity in sentencing
                e.   police would be in danger
                f.   prison population already houses highest-frequency criminal

IX.   Policy implications of choice theory
          1.   has had an important impact on crime prevention
          2.   development of the just desert position

X.   Summary

MULTIPLE CHOICE

1. Rational choice theory has its roots in the classical school of criminology developed by
    a. Lombroso.
    2. Beccaria.
    3. Durkheim.
    4. Marx.

2. Rational choice theory dovetails with _____ theory.
    a. biological trait
    b. social learning
    c. routine activities
    d. cognitive development

3. Crime is said to be _____ from the rational choice perspective because criminals evaluate the characteristics to determine their suitability.
    a. offense-specific
    b. offender-specific
    c. target-specific
    d. choice-specific

4. Clarke and Harris found that _____ are very selective in their choice of targets.
    a. burglars
    b. murderers
    c. arsonists
    d. auto thieves

5. Jacobs found that drug dealers use specific techniques to avoid being apprehended by police. They play what they call the _____ before dealing drugs.
    a. "sneak peak game"
    b. "deal game"
    c. "cop shop game"
    d. "peep game"

6. Some law violators describe the "adrenaline rush" that comes from successfully executing illegal activities in dangerous situations. This has been termed
    a. the rush.
    b. edgework.
    c. "doin'good."
    d. "sneaky thrills."

7. Situational crime prevention was first popularized in the U.S. by
    a. Beccaria.
    b. Clarke and Harris.
    c. Katz.
    d. Newman.

8. Crime-reduction programs may produce a short-term positive effect, but benefits dissipate as criminals adjust to new conditions. This creates the problem of
    a. displacement.
    b. extinction.
    c. diffusion of benefits.
    d. encouragement.

9. _____ occurs when crime control efforts in one locale reduce crime in other nontarget areas.
    a. Displacement

  b. Extinction

  c. Diffusion of benefits

  d. Encouragement

10. Research shows that when the number of arrests increase, the number of index crimes reported to police declines the next

  a. day.

  b. week.

  c. month.

  d. year.

11. A recent initiative by the Dallas Police Department to aggressively pursue _____ and curfew enforcement resulted in lower rates of gang violence.

  a. burglary

  b. auto theft

  c. truancy

  d. vandalism

12. The basis of _____ theory is that potential criminals may begin to model their behavior after state authorities.

  a. execution

  b. brutalization effect

  c. social learning

  d. punishment

13. Anticrime campaigns have been designed to play on

  a. fear of crime.

  b. fear of arrest.

  c. fear of shame.

  d. fear of conviction.

14. Research on repeat sexual offenders finds that they suffer from a/an _____ that negates the deterrent effect of law.

  a. lack of conscious

  b. mental disorder

  c. elevated emotional state

  d. elevated level of testosterone

15. The American legal system is not very effective. Only _____ of all serious offenses result in apprehension.

  a. 10

  b. 15

  c. 20

  d. 25

16. The odds of receiving a prison term are less than _____ per 1000 crimes committed.

  a. 20

  b. 30

  c. 40

  d. 50

17. In the _____ approach, the offenders' evil deeds are condemned while, at the same time, efforts are made to reconnect them to their neighbors, friends, and family.

  a. stigmatization

  b. labeling

  c. general deterrence

   d. reintegrative shaming

18. A strict incarceration policy would result in a growing number of elderly inmates whose maintenance costs are _____ times higher per year than those of younger inmates.
   a. one
   b. two
   c. three
   d. four

19. Criminologists oppose habitual offender laws for several reasons. Which of the following is not one of those reasons?
   a. Current sentences for violent crime are already quite severe.
   b. There would be racial disparity.
   c. Most three-time losers are juveniles.
   d. An expanding prison population will drive up already high prison costs.

20. The _____ suggests that retribution justifies punishment because people deserve what they get for past deeds.
   a. three strikes and you're out policy
   b. brutalization effect
   c. crime elimination model
   d. just desert model

TRUE/FALSE

1. Beccaria's approach was to "let the punishment fit the criminal."

2. Criminals appear to be more rational and have more self-control than other people.

3. According to the rational choice approach, the decision to commit crime, regardless of its substance, is structured by three factors.

4. Evidence indicates that theft crimes do not appear to be rational.

5. Oscar Newman coined the term defensible space.

6. Diffusion of benefits occurs when efforts to prevent one crime unintentionally prevent another.

7. According to the rational choice view, motivated people will violate the law if left free and unrestricted.

8. Most research shows that the likelihood of being arrested or imprisoned has a great deterrent effect on crime.

9. There is little consensus that strict punishment alone can reduce criminal activities.

10. Research conducted in various nations has found that homicide rates decline after capital punishment is abolished.

11. Studies measuring the perception of punishment agree that the certainty of punishment has a greater deterrent effect than its severity.

12. Research shows that the overall probability of rearrest decreases following incarceration.

13. The concept of reintegrative shaming is a key component of the restorative justice movement.

14. The more prior incarceration experiences inmates have, the more likely they are to recidivate within 12 months of their release.

15. Most three-time losers are at the verge of aging out of crime.

FILL-IN REVIEW

1. Becarria believed that criminals weigh the _____ and _____ of crime before choosing to violate the law.

2. Crime is said to _____-_____ because criminals evaluate the characteristics of targets to determine their suitability.

3. Criminal choice involves such actions as choosing the place of crime, selecting targets, and learning _____ _____.

4. Theft crimes appear _____ because thieves and burglars typically choose targets that present little risk and plan their attacks carefully.

5. Crime is _____. People may rationally choose crime because it provides them with psychological and social benefits.

6. _____ crime prevention efforts are designed to reduce or redirect crime by making it more difficult to profit from illegal acts.

7. _____ _____ models are based on the fear of punishment.

8. _____ _____ aims at reducing crime through the application of severe punishments.

9. _____ _____ are designed to reduce crime by taking known criminals out of circulation, preventing them from having the opportunity to commit further offenses.

10. The _____ _____ position has been most clearly spelled out by criminologist Andrew Von Hirsch.

11. The just desert model suggests that _____ justifies punishment.

12. _____ theory has been influential in shaping public policy.

13. _____ _____ strategies are designed to reduce the value of crime to the potential criminal.

14. According to _____ theory, if the certainty of arrest, conviction, and sanctioning

15. Some experts believe that the purpose of the law and justice system is to create a " _____ _____."

ESSAYS

1. There is evidence that even seemingly "unplanned' street crimes may be the product of careful risk assessment. Discuss what the research tells us about the rationality involved in armed robbery and in drug use.

2. Situational crime prevention tactics generally fall into one of four categories. Discuss two of these.

3. Discuss the differences between general and specific deterrence views.

4. Explain why Braithwaite argues that crime control can be achieved more effectively through a policy of reintegrative shaming.

5. Summarize and discuss Andrew Von Hisch's views.

CHAPTER 4 ANSWER SECTION

MULTIPLE CHOICE

1. b
2. c
3. a
4. d
5. d
6. b
7. d
8. b
9. c
10. a
11. c
12. b
13. c
14. c
15. a
16. a
17. d
18. c
19. c
20. d

TRUE/FALSE

1. F
2. F
3. T
4. F
5. T
6. T
7. T
8. F
9. T
10. T
11. T
12. F
13. T
14. T
15. T

FILL-IN REVIEW

1. benefits, consequences
2. offense-specific
3. criminal techniques
4. rational
5. seductive
6. Situational
7. General deterrence
8. Specific deterrence
9. Incapacitation strategies
10. just desert
11. retribution
12. Choice
13. Target reduction
14. deterrence
15. threat system

5   *Trait Theory: It's in Their Blood*

LEARNING OBJECTIVES

After covering the material in this chapter, you should understand:

1. the two major categories of trait theories: biological makeup and psychological functioning.

2. that contemporary trait theorists focus on basic human behavior and drives that are linked to antisocial behavior patterns.

3. why trait theories have recently gained prominence.

4. how biochemical conditions are thought to influence antisocial behavior.

5. the relationship between hormones and aggressive behavior.

6. the effect of environmental contaminants on emotional and behavioral disorders.

7. the relationship between neurological dysfunction and crime.

8. that one biosocial theme is that the human traits associated with criminality have a genetic basis.

9. crime rate differences between the genders may be a matter of inherent differences in mating patterns.

10. questions raised by biological perspectives on crime.

11. psychodynamic approaches toward abnormal behavior, mental illness, and crime.

12. basic assumptions of social learning theory.

13. why information-processing theory has been used to explain the occurrence of date rape.

14. research efforts that have attempted to identify criminal personality traits.

15. the nature versus nurture debate.

16. how biological and psychological views of criminality have influenced crime control and prevention policy.

KEYWORDS

trait theory
sociobiology
equipotentiality
hypoglycemia
androgens
testosterone
premenstrual syndrome (PMS)
neurophysiology
minimal brain dysfunction (MBD)
attention deficit/hyperactivity disorder (ADHD)
neurotransmitters

arousal theory
monozygotic (MZ) twins
dizygotic (DZ) twins
cheater theory
psychodynamic
psychoanalytic
id
ego
superego
neurotic
psychotic
disorder
schizophrenia
latent delinquincy
bipolar disorder
behavior theory
social learning
behavior modeling
cognitive theory
information-processing theory
personality
antisocial personality
nature theory
nurture theory
primary prevention programs
secondary prevention programs

CHAPTER OUTLINE

I.   The development of trait theory
    1.   two major categories: biological and psychological
    2.   view began with the early research of Lombroso
        a.   this work not regarded as scientific fact today
    3.   biological explanations of crime remerged in the 1970s
    4.   sociobiology stresses that biological and genetic conditions affect how social behaviors are learned and perceived
    5.   sociobiologists view biology, environment, and learning as mutually interdependent factors

II.   Contemporary trait theories
    1.   do not suggest a single biological or psychological attribute explains all criminality
    2.   focus is on basic human behavior and drives that are linked to antisocial behavior

III. Biological trait theories
    1.   focus on biological conditions that control human behavior
    2.   researchers referred to as biocriminologists, biosocial criminologist, or biologically oriented criminologists
    A.   Biochemical conditions and crime
    1.   belief that biochemical conditions influence antisocial behavior
        a.   the "Twinkie defense" illustrates this view
    2.   maintains that minimal levels of minerals and chemicals are needed for normal brain functioning and growth
    3.   studies link hypoglycemia to outbursts of antisocial behavior and violence
    4.   research has found that abnormal levels of male sex hormones produce aggressive behavior

a. gender differences in the crime rate may be explained by differences in androgen levels

b. the debate over the link between PMS and crime still exists

5. recent research has linked lead ingestion to problem behavior

6. relationship between neurological dysfunction and crime first received attention in 1968

    a. Charles Whitman killings

    b. chronic violent offenders have higher levels of brain dysfunction than general population

    c. minimal brain dysfunction can be manifested in episodic periods of explosive rage

    d. research studies have linked the onset and maintenance of a delinquent career to ADHD

    e. recent studies of violent criminals show that low serotonin levels are associated with poor impulse control and hyperactivity

    f. arousal theory argues that people's brains function differently in response to environmental stimuli

B. Genetics and crime

1. human traits associated with criminality have a genetic basis

    a. abnormal XYY chromosomal structure

2. there is no certainty about the relationship between parental and child deviance but part of the association might be genetic

3. findings of twin and adoption studies tentatively support a genetic basic for criminality

C. Evolutionary views of crime

1. human traits that produce violence and aggression have been advanced by the long process of human evolution

2. gender difference in violence rates are based loosely on mammalian mating patterns

    a. this may account for differences in crime rates between the genders

3. according to cheater theory, a subpopulation of men has evolved with genes that incline them toward low parental involvement

D. Evaluation of the biological branch of trait theory

1. biosocial perspectives on crime have raised challenging questions

2. some theories viewed as racist and dysfunctional

3. problems exist with geographic, social, and temporal patterns in crime rate

4. lack of empirical testing

IV. Psychological trait theories

1. focus on the psychological aspects of crime

2. Goring and Tarde were pioneers in this area

A. Psychodynamic perspective

1. originated by Freud

    a. three-part structure of personality: id, ego, and superego

2. most serious disorder is schizophrenia

3. criminals viewed as id-dominated persons who suffer one or more disorder

4. criminal offender depicted as aggressive, frustrated person dominated by events that occurred early in childhood

5. offenders have various mood and behavior disorders

6. suggest a linkage between mental illness and crime

B. Behavioral perspective: social learning theory

1. maintains that human actions are developed through learning experiences

2. branch most relevant to criminology is social learning theory

    a. people are not born with ability to act violently, they learn to be aggressive through their life experiences

3. view violence as something learned through a process called behavior modeling

4. aggressive acts modeled after three principal sources:

                      a.   family interaction
                      b.   environmental interaction
                      c.   mass media
              5.   four factors may contribute to violent or aggressive behavior
                      a.   an event that heightens arousal
                      b.   aggressive skills
                      c.   expected outcomes
                      d.   consistency of behavior

C.   Cognitive theory
    1.   information-processing focuses on how people process, store, encode, retrieve, and manipulate information to make decisions and solve problems
    2.   information-processing theory used to explain the occurrence of date rape

D.   Personality and crime
    1.   research efforts have attempted to identify criminal personality traits
    2.   a number of personality deficits have been identified in the criminal population
            a.   antisocial personality
    3.   root causes of crime may be found in forces that influence early human development

E.   Intelligence and crime
    1.   early criminologists claimed delinquents and criminals have below-average IQ
    2.   proponents of nature theory argue that intelligence is largely determined genetically
    3.   proponents of nurture theory argue that intelligence is not inherited
            a.   intelligence is partly biological but primarily sociological
            b.   Sutherland's study put the IQ-crime link to an end
            c.   IQ-crime link became important again due to research by Hirsch and Handling
            d.   Bernstein and Murray firmly advocate IQ-crime link
    4.   unlikely the IQ-criminality debate will be settled soon

VI.   Social policy implications
    1.   biological and psychological views of criminality had influence on crime control and prevention policy in the twentieth century
            a.   primary prevention programs
            b.   secondary prevention programs

V.   Summary

MUTLIPLE CHOICE

1. Sociobiology differs from earlier theories of behavior in that it stresses that biological and _____ conditions affect how social behaviors are learned and perceived.
   a. social
   b. psychological
   c. genetic
   d. All of the above.

2. Sociobiologists view biology, environment, and _____ as mutually interdependent factors.
   a. learning
   b. socialization
   c. gender
   d. psychology

3. Early criminologists such as _____ suggested that some people had crime-producing biological traits.
   a. Beccaria
   b. Lombroso
   c. Durkheim
   d. Bentham

4. Biocriminologists maintain that minimal levels of _____ and chemicals are needed for normal brain functioning and growth, especially during the early years of life.
   a. vitamins
   b. minerals
   c. androgens
   d. vegetables

5. _____ occurs when blood glucose falls below levels necessary for normal and efficient brain functioning.
   a. Glugoglycemia
   b. Glucosis
   c. Hypoglycemia
   d. Hypocosis

6. _____, the most abundant androgen, which control secondary sex characteristics, has been linked to criminality.
   a. Estrogen
   b. Progesterone
   c. Testosterone
   d. Steroid

7. Ingestion of _____ may help explain why hyperactive children manifest conduct problems and antisocial behavior.
   a. minerals
   b. vitamins
   c. zinc
   d. lead

8. Some researchers focus their attention on the study of _____, or the study of brain activity.
   a. neurosis
   b. neurophysiology
   c. neuropsychology
   d. neurobiology

9. MBD stands for
    a. maximum brain disorder.
    b. minimum brain disorder.
    c. maximum brain dysfunction.
    d. minimum brain dysfunction.

10. Research studies now link _____ to the onset and maintenance of a delinquent career.
    a. ADHD
    b. PMS
    c. MBD
    d. BCN

11. _____ are chemical compounds that influence or activate brain functions.
    a. Androgens
    b. Brain chemistry neurotransmitters
    c. Hormones
    d. Neurophysical compounds

12. According to the _____ view of crime, the competition for scarce resources has influenced and shaped the human species.
    a. evolutionary
    b. behavior
    c. biochemical
    d. cheater

13. Evolutionary concepts that have been linked to _____ differences in violence rates are based loosely on mammalian mating patterns.
    a. societal
    b. racial
    c. gender
    d. cultural

14. According to this theory, a subpopulation of men has evolved with genes that incline them toward extremely low parental involvement.
    a. evolutionary
    b. arousal
    c. biochemical
    d. cheater

15. According to Freud's version of _____ theory, the human personality has a three-part structure.
    a. social learning
    b. psychodynamic
    c. cognitive
    d. personality

16. Psychodynamic theorists originally used the term _____ to refer to people who experienced feelings of mental anguish and feared they were losing control of their personalities.
    a. psychotic
    b. crazy
    c. abnormal
    d. neurotic

17. The major premise of _____ theory is that people alter their behavior according to the reactions it receives from others.
    a. evolutionary
    b. behavior

     c. biochemical

     d. cheater

18. Information-processing theory is actually a _____ theory.
     a. nature
     b. social learning
     c. personality
     d. cognitive

19. Proponents of _____ theory argue that intelligence is largely determined genetically, that ancestry determines IQ, and that low intelligence, as demonstrated by low IQ, is linked to criminal behavior.
     a. nature
     b. nurture
     c. personality
     d. cognitive

20. Proponents of _____ theory argue that intelligence is not inherited and low-IQ parents do not necessarily produce low-IQ children.
     a. nature
     b. nurture
     c. personality
     d. cognitive

TRUE/FALSE

1. It is suspected that a single trait is responsible for all crime.

2. Almost all empirical research has supported the argument that there is a link between sugar consumption and violence.

3. Research studies have linked hypoglycemia to outbursts of antisocial behavior and violence.

4. Biosocial research has found that abnormal levels of estrogen produce aggressive behavior in males.

5. The link between PMS and delinquency was first popularized more than 30 years ago.

6. The Whitman case brought attention to the association between neurological impairment and crime.

7. Low serotonin levels have been associated with poor impulse control and hyperactivity.

8. There is strong empirical evidence about the relationship between parental and child deviance.

9 Critics of the biosocial perspectives on crime find some of these theories racist and dysfunctional.

10. Since Freud's original research, psychoanalysts have continued to view criminals as ego-dominated persons who suffer from one or more disorders that render them incapable of controlling impulsive, pleasure-seeking drives.

11. Empirical evidence suggests a strong linkage between mental illness and crime.

12. Social learning theorists view violence as something learned through a process called behavior modeling.

13. Information-processing theory has been used to explain the occurrence of robbery.

14. Primary prevention programs provide treatment such as psychological counseling to youths and adults after they have violated the law.

15. Psychological attempts to explain criminal behavior have historical roots in the concept that all criminals are insane or mentally damaged.

FILL-IN REVIEW

1. Some contemporary criminologists believe that human traits interact with _____ factors to produce criminal behaviors.

2. The male hormone _____ is linked to criminality.

3. _____ holds that violence-producing traits are passed on from generation to generation.

4. Biological explanations fail to account for the _____. _____, and _____ patterns in the crime rate.

5. According to _____ theory, instinctual drives developed over thousands of years of human history control behavior. The urge to procreate influences male violence.

6. According to _____ theory, unconscious motivations developed early in childhood propel some people into destructive or illegal behavior.

7. _____ view aggression as a learned behavior.

8. Cognitive theory stresses _____ and _____.

9. The early positivist criminologists were_____.

10. The equal potential to learn and achieve is referred to as _____.

11. Some trait theorists believe that biochemical conditions, including those that are genetically predetermined and those that are acquired through _____ and _____ influence antisocial behavior.

12. Levels of _____ decline during the life cycle, which may explain why violence rates diminish over time.

13. Not all research efforts have found that _____ twin pairs are more closely related in their criminal behavior then _____ or ordinary sibling pairs, and some have found an association that is at best modest.

14. The most serious disorder is _____, marked by hearing nonexistent voices, seeing hallucinations, and exhibiting inappropriate responses.

15. When cognitive theorists who study information processing try to explain antisocial behavior, they do so in terms of _____ _____ and how people use information to understand their environment.

ESSAY QUESTIONS

1. Contemporary trait theorists do not suggest that a single biological or psychological attribute adequately explains all criminality. What, then, do they focus on?

2. Biosocial theorists note that males are biologically and naturally more aggressive then females, whereas women are more nurturing toward the young. This discrepancy has been linked to gender-based hormonal differences. How do biosocial theorists explain gender-differences in aggressive behavior?

3. Discuss the link between brain chemistry and crime.

4. Discuss the psychodynamics of criminal behavior.

5. Discuss the arguments put forth by proponents of nature theory. The well-written answer will include specific research from the text.

CHAPTER 5 ANSWER SECTION

MULTIPLE CHOICE

1. c
2. a.
3. b
4. b
5. c
6. c
7. d
8. b
9. c
10. a
11. b
12. a
13. c
14. d
15. b
16. d
17. b
18. d
19. a
20. b

TRUE/FALSE

1. F
2. F
3. T
4. F
5. T
6. T
7. T
8. F
9. T
10. F
11. F
12. T
13. F
14. F
15. T

FILL-IN REVIEW

1. environmental
2. testosterone
3. Genetic
4. geographic, social, temporal
5. evolutionary
6. psychodynamic
7. Behaviorists
8. knowing, perception
9. biologists
10. equipotentiality
11. diet, environment
12. testosterone
13. MZ,DZ
14. schizophrenia
15. mental perception

6 Social Structure Theory: Because They're Poor

LEANING OBJECTIVES

After covering material in this chapter, you should understand:

1. the impact of the economic structure on children in the U.S.

2. the culture of poverty concept.

3. how disadvantaged economic class position is viewed as a primary cause of crime.

4. the differences between social disorganization, strain, cultural deviance, subculture, and cultural transmission theories.

5. the legacy of Shaw and McKay.

6. why recent social ecological research is important.

7. Merton's modes of social adaptation.

8. the strengths and weaknesses of anomie theory.

9. the concept of relative deprivation and how it applies to crime.

10. the basic assumptions of general strain theory, and its evaluation.

11. the basic assumptions of cultural deviance theory, and explanations it offers for delinquent subcultures.

12. Cohen's approach to delinquent subcultures.

13. the concept of differential opportunity and how it relates to delinquency.

14. the impact of social structure theory on social policy.

KEYWORDS

stratified
social class
culture of poverty
at-risk
underclass
truly disadvantaged
social structure theory
social disorganization theory
strain theory
strain
cultural deviance theory
subculture
cultural transmission
transitional neighborhood

concentration effect
collective efficiency
social altruism
anomie
anomie theory
institutional anomie theory
American Dream
relative deprivation
general strain theory (GST)
negative affective states
focal concerns
delinquent subculture
status frustration
middle-class measuring rods
reaction formation
differential opportunity

CHAPTER OUTLINE

I.   Economic structure and crime
        1. people in the U.S. live in a stratified society
            a. in U.S. society, it is common to identify people as upper, middle, or lower class
            b. 36 million people live below the poverty line
        2. children are hit hard by poverty
            a. poor children are less likely to do well in school
            b. poor children suffer more health problems
        3. adolescents in the worst neighborhoods have the greatest risk of dropping out of school and becoming teenage parents
        4. Hispanic and African American children are more than twice as likely to be poor as Asian and European American children

II.   Lower-class culture
        1. slum areas produce a culture of poverty passed from one generation to the next
        2. the underclass is cut off from society
            a. burdens of underclass life are most often felt by minority group members
            b. up to half of all minority males are under criminal justice system control
            c. many of the underclass are African American children

III.   Social structure theories
        1. many criminologists view disadvantaged economic class position as a primary cause of crime
            a. social structure theories take this view
        2. three independent yet overlapping branches of social structure theory
            a. social disorganization theory focuses on urban conditions that affect crime rates
            b. strain theory holds that crime is a function of conflict between people's goals and the means they use to obtain them
            c. cultural deviance theory combines elements of strain and social disorganization theories

IV.   Social disorganization theory
        1. links crime rates to neighborhood ecological characteristics
        2. views crime-ridden neighborhoods as those in which population is transient
    A. The work of Shaw and McKay

1. Chicago sociologists who linked life in transitional slum areas to the inclination to commit crime
2. explained crime and delinquency within the context of the changing urban environment and ecological development of the city
    a. transitional neighborhoods suffered high rates of population turnover; residents did not remain to defend the neighborhoods against crime
3. identified nine concentric zones in the Chicago
    a. heaviest crime concentration was in the transitional inner-city zones
4. found a stable pattern of criminal activity in the nine zones over 65 years
    a. rates were always highest in zones I and II
5. social disorganization concepts are still prominent within criminology
6. most important findings were that crime rates correspond to neighborhood structure and that crime is created by destructive ecological conditions in urban slums

B. The social ecology school
1. contemporary social ecologists emerged in the 1980s
2. recent social ecological research has focused on:
    a. community disorganization
    b. poverty and unemployment
    c. community fear
    d. community change
    e. poverty concentration
    f. weak social controls
    g. social support/altruism

V. Strain theories
1. view crime as a direct result of lower-class frustration and anger
2. believe most people share similar goals and values

A. Theory of anomie
1. Merton developed a theory of anomie
2. he argues that in the U.S., legitimate means to acquire wealth are stratified across class and status lines
3. criminal or delinquent solutions may be seen as a means of attaining goals
4. varieties of social adaptations
    a. conformity
    b. innovation
    c. ritualism
    d. retreatism
    e. rebellion
5. this view of anomie has been enduring and influential
6. theory has been criticized for:
    a. not explaining why people choose to commit certain types of crime
    b. not explaining why most young criminals desist from crime as adults

B. Institutional anomie theory
1. developed by Messner and Rosenfeld
2. argues that anomie pervades American culture
    a. institutions that might otherwise control exaggerated emphasis on financial success have been rendered powerless or obsolete
    b. these social institutions have been undermined in three ways:
        1. noneconomic functions and roles have been devalued
        2. noneconomic roles become subordinate to and must accommodate economic roles when conflicts emerge
        3. economic language, standards, and norms penetrate into noneconomic realms
3. the relatively high American crime rates can be explained by the interrelationship between culture and institutions

C. Relative deprivation theory

             1. concept was proposed by Judith Blau and Peter Blau
             2. concept combines concepts from anomie theory with those found in social disorganization models
             3. relative deprivation is felt most acutely by African Americans youths
             4. people who perceive themselves as economically deprived relative to people they know, as well as to society, may be motivated to commit deviant and criminal behaviors

D. General strain theory (GST)
             1. developed by Agnew
             2. identifies micro- or individual-level influences of strain
             3. attempts to offer a more general explanation of criminal activity among all elements of society rather than just the lower classes
             4. multiple sources of strain:
                 a. failure to achieve positively valued goals
                 b. disjunction of expectations and achievements
                 c. removal of positively valued stimuli
                 d. presentation of negative stimuli
             5. there is empirical support for GST theory

VI. Cultural deviance theory
             1. combines the effects of social disorganization and strain to explain how people living in deteriorated neighborhoods react to social isolation and economic deprivation
             2. more than 40 years ago, Walter Miller identified conduct norms, known as focal concerns that help define lower-class culture

A. Theory of delinquent subcultures
             1. articulated by Cohen in 1955
             2. central position was that delinquent behavior of lower-class youths is a protest against norms and values of middle-class U.S. culture
             3. the delinquent subculture is a consequence of socialization practices in lower-class environments
             4. standards set by authority figures are called middle-class measuring rods
             5. three existing subcultures:
                 a. the corner boy
                 b. the college boy
                 c. the delinquent boy
             6. this approach integrates strain and social disorganization theories

B. Theory of differential opportunity
             1. developed by Cloward and Ohlin
             2. centerpiece of the theory is concept of differential opportunity
             3. all opportunities for success, both illegal and conventional, are closed for the most disadvantaged youths
             4. young people likely to join one of thee types of gangs because of differential opportunity:
                 a. criminal gangs
                 b. conflict gangs
                 c. retreatist gangs
             5. theory integrates cultural deviance and social disorganization variables

VI. Social structure theory and social policy
             1. social structure theory had influenced social policy
             2. efforts have been made to reduce crime by improving community structure in inner-city high-crime areas
             3. social structure concepts were a critical ingredient in the Kennedy and Johnson administrations' War on Poverty

VII. Summary

MULTIPLE CHOICE

1. People in the United States live in a _____ society.
   a. caste
   b. socialist
   c. stratified
   d. communistic

2. In _____ sociologist Oscar Lewis coined the phrase "culture of poverty."
   a. 1956
   b. 1966
   c. 1976
   d. 1986

3. Up to a _____ of all minority males are under the justice system control
   a. third
   b. fourth
   c. fifth
   d. half

4. The social structure theory views _____ as a primary cause of crime.
   a. disadvantaged economic position
   b. biological makeup
   c. low self-control
   d. low intelligence

5. The social structure perspective encompasses three independent branches of theory. Which of the following is not one of these theories?
   a. strain
   b. cultural deviance
   c. Marxist
   d. social disorganization

6. The statement, "urban conditions affect crime rates," is reflective of which theory?
   a. strain
   b. cultural deviance
   c. Marxist
   d. social disorganization

7. The statement, "crime is a function of the conflict between people's goals and the means they use to obtain them," if reflective of which theory?
   a. strain
   b. cultural deviance
   c. Marxist
   d. social disorganization

8. Because crime rates are higher in lower-class areas, many criminologist believe that the cause of crime is rooted in _____ factors.
   a. intelligence
   b. socioeconomic
   c. biological
   d. All of the above.

9. Subcultural values are handed down from one generation to the next in a process called
   a. enculturation.
   b. inheritance.

c. cultural transmission.

d. subcultural transmission.

10. Shaw and McKay began their work on Chicago crime during the early
   a. 1920s.
   b. 1930s.
   c. 1940s.
   d. 1950s.

11. Shaw and McKay's statistical analysis confirmed that even though _____ changed, the highest crime rates were always in zones I and II.
   a. ethnic groups
   b. crime rates
   c. weather
   d. the number of juveniles

12. One of the most important of Shaw and McKay's findings was that crime is created by destructive _____ in urban slums.
   a. juveniles
   b. adults
   c. ecological conditions
   d. police

13. In the 1980s, a group of criminologists continued studying ecological conditions, reviving concern about the effects of
   a. cultural transmission.
   b. social disorganization.
   c. cultural deviance.
   d. socialization.

14. Which of the following is not a sign of physical incivility?
   a. trash and litter
   b. abandoned storefronts
   c. burned-out buildings
   d. vagabonds

15. According to Merton, _____ gain pleasure from practicing traditional ceremonies regardless of whether they have a real purpose or a goal.
   a. rebels
   b. conformists
   c. ritualists
   d. innovators

16. According to the _____ concept, people who perceive themselves as economically deprived relative to people they know may begin to form feelings of negativity and hostility.
   a. relative deprivation
   b. anomie
   c. culture of poverty
   d. cultural deviance

17. According to _____, clinging to lower-class focal concerns promotes illegal or violent behavior.
   a. Merton
   b. Agnew
   c. Cohen
   d. Miller

55

KVCC KALAMAZOO VALLEY COMMUNITY COLLEGE LIBRARY

18. _____ first articulated the theory of delinquent subcultures in 1955.
    a. Merton
    b. Agnew
    c. Cohen
    d. Miller

19. According to this concept, people in all strata of society share the same success goals; however, those in the lower class have limited means of achieving them.
    a. differential opportunity
    b. anomie
    c. reaction formation
    d. status frustration

20. The best-known strain theory is Merton's theory of
    a. status frustration.
    b. anomie.
    c. differential opportunity.
    d. social disorganization.

TRUE/FALSE

1. Wilson has labeled those members of the lowest level of the underclass as the truly disadvantaged.

2. Social structure theorists view the real crime problem as essentially a lower-class phenomenon.

3. Strain theories combine elements of both social disorganization and cultural deviance theories.

4. Shaw and McKay found that crime rates fluctuated dramatically in the nine ecological zones over a 65 year period.

5. Research indicates that the presence of fear incites more crime.

6. The concentration effect supports, in some measure, Shaw and McKay's position.

7. Strain theory holds that destructive social forces present in inner-city areas control human behavior and promote crime.

8. Merton argues that in the United Sates, legitimate means to acquire wealth are stratified across class and status lines.

9. One of the strengths of Merton's theory is that he explains why people choose t commit certain types of crime.

10. Sociologist Agnew's GST is a micro-level theory.

11. There is little empirical support for GST.

12. Miller's central position was that delinquent behavior of lower-class youths is actually a protest against the norms and values of middle-class U.S. culture.

13. According to Cohen, the development of the delinquent subculture is a consequence of socialization practices in lower-class environments.

14. Cloward and Ohlin combined strain and social disorganization principles to portray a gang-sustaining criminal subculture.

15. Criminal gangs develop in communities unable to provide either legitimate or illegitimate opportunities according to Cloward and Ohlin.

FILL-IN REVIEW

1. Some criminologists believe that _____ _____ _____ in poverty areas are responsible for high crime rates.

2. Despite economic headway, there are still more than _____ million indigent Americans.

3. _____ _____ theory holds that destructive social forces present in inner-city areas control human behavior and promote crime.

4. _____ and _____ first identified the concepts central to social disorganization.

5. The _____ _____ school associates community deterioration and economic decline with crime rates.

6. GST is not solely a _____ _____ since it recognizes non-class-related sources of strain.

7. Strain theories hold that _____ _____ causes frustration, which leads to crime.

8. Messner and Rosenfeld's _____ _____ theory argues that the goal of success at all costs has invaded every aspect of American life.

9. _____ general theory of strain suggests that there is more than one source of anomie.

10. According to Millers, clinging to _____-_____ _____ promotes illegal or violent behavior.

11. Cohen calls the standards set by authority figures in the U.S. _____-_____ _____ _____.

12. According to Cohen, the _____ boy role is the most common response to middle-class rejection.

13. According to Cohen, the _____ boy embraces the cultural and social values of the middle class.

14. The centerpiece of the Cloward and Ohlin theory is the concept of _____ _____.

15. According to Cloward and Ohlin, _____ are double failures, unable to gain success through legitimate means and unwilling to do so through illegal ones.

ESSAY QUESTIONS

1. Cloward and Ohlin claimed that because of differential opportunity, young people are likely to join one of three types of gangs. Discuss each type of gang.

2. According to Cohen, the development of the delinquent subculture is a consequence of socialization practices in lower-class environments. Discuss what Cohen means when he states this.

3. Messner and Rosenfeld theory's is an updating of Mertn's work. Discuss this theory.

4. Discuss the strengths and weaknesses of Merton's anomie theory.

5. Explain why Agnew's GST is not solely a cultural deviance theory.

CHAPTER 6 ANSWER SECTION

MULTIPLE CHOICE

1.   c
2.   b
3.   d
4.   a
5.   c
6.   d
7.   a
8.   b
9.   d
10.   a
11.   b
12.   c
13.   b
14.   d
15.   c
16.   a
17.   d
18.   c
19.   a
20.   b

TRUE/FALSE

1.   T
2.   T
3.   F
4.   F
5.   T
6.   F
7.   F
8.   T
9.   F
10.   T
11.   F
12.   F
13.   T
14.   T
15.   F

FILL-IN REVIEW

1.   destructive social forces
2.   30
3.   Social disorganization
4.   Shaw, McKay
5.   social ecology
6.   cultural deviance
7.   economic deprivation
8.   institutional anomie
9.   Agnew's
10.   lower-class focal
11.   middle-class measuring rods
12.   corner
13.   college
14.   differential opportunity
15.   retreatists

7 *Social Process Theories: Socialized to Crime*

LEARNING OBJECTIVES

After covering material in this chapter, you should understand:

1. the view of crime referred to as social process theory.

2. the impact of family relations, educational experience, and peer relations on crime.

3. the relationship between institutional involvement and belief, and crime.

4. the similarities and differences between the three branches of the social process approach.

5. social theorists believe that crime is a product of learning norms, values, and behaviors associated with criminal activity.

6. why Sutherland's differential association theory is prominent.

7. the concepts of neutralization theory.

8. that social control theorists maintain that all people have the potential to violate the law and that modern society presents many opportunities for illegal activity.

9. Hirschi's social control theory, and the impact of social bonds on the decision to commit crime.

10. that social reaction (labeling) theory explains criminal careers in terms of destructive interactions and stigma-producing encounters.

11. the differences between primary and secondary deviance.

12. the impact of social process theories on social policy.

13. the strengths and weaknesses of each of the above theories.

KEYWORDS

socialization
social process theory
social learning theory
social control theory
social reaction theory (labeling theory)
differential association theory
culture conflict
neutralization theory
drift
neutralization techniques
self-control
commitment to conformity
social bond
stigmatize
moral entrepreneur
reflective role-taking

retrospective reading
primary deviance
secondary deviance
deviance amplification
contextual discrimination
diversion programs
restitution

CHAPTER OUTLINE

I.   Socialization and crime
- 1.   social process theories believe that criminality is a function of individual socialization
- 2.   social process theories share one basic concept:
  - a.   all people have the potential to become delinquents or criminals
- 3.   these theories have endured because the relationship between social class and crime is still uncertain
  - A.   Family relations
    - 1.   considered a major determinant of behavior
    - 2.   many criminologists discount the association between family structure and the onset of criminality
  - B.   Educational experience
    - 1.   educational process and adolescent school achievement have been linked to criminality
  - C.   Peer relations
    - 1.   peer groups affect human conduct and influence decision making behavior choices
    - 2.   delinquent peers exert tremendous influence on behavior, attitudes, and beliefs
    - 3.   criminal activity diminishes as peer influence diminishes
  - D.   Institutional involvement and belief
    - 1.   Hirschi and Stark found that the association between religious attendance or belief and delinquent behavior patterns were negligible
    - 2.   recent studies find the opposite
  - E.   The effects of socialization on crime
    - 1.   positive self-image, strong moral values, and support from parents, peers, teachers, neighbors lead to a positive self-image

III.   Social learning theories
- 1.   crime is a product of learning the norms, values, and behaviors associated with criminal activity
  - A.   Differential association theory
    - 1.   developed by Edwin Sutherand, explained and popularized by Cressey
    - 2.   crime is a function of the learning process
    - 3.   basic principles:
      - a.   criminal behavior is learned
      - b.   criminal behavior is learned as a byproduct of interacting with others
      - c.   this learning occurs within intimate personal groups
      - d.   this learning involves assimilating techniques of committing crime
      - e.   specific direction of motives and drives is learned from perceptions of the legal code as favorable or unfavorable
      - f.   person becomes a criminal when he or she perceives more favorable than unfavorable consequences of violating the law
      - g.   differential associations may vary in frequency, duration, priority, and intensity
      - h.   this process of learning is the same as any other learning process
      - i.   motives for criminal behavior cannot logically be the same as those for conventional behavior

4. research involving assumptions has been sparse
   a. principles are difficult to conceptualize
5 some research efforts have supported the core principles of the theory
6. important theory since it does not specify that criminals come from a disorganized area or are members of the lower class
7. criticisms:
   a. fails to account for the origin of criminal definitions
   b. assumes criminal and delinquent acts to be rational and systematic
   c. vagueness of terms make it difficult to test

B. Neutralization theory
1. identified with the writings of Matza and Sykes
2. views the process of becoming a criminal as a learning experience
3. points out that even the most committed criminals and delinquents are not involved in criminality all the time
4. justifications for law-violating behavior:
   a. criminals sometimes voice guilt over their illegal acts
   b. offenders often respect and admire honest, law-abiding persons
   c. criminals define whom they can victimize
   d. criminals are not immune to the demands of conformity
5. techniques of neutralization:
   a. denial of responsibility
   b. denial of injury
   c. denial of the victim
   d. condemnation of the condemners
   e. appeal to higher loyalties
6. results to test the theory empirically have been inconclusive

C. Are learning theories valid?
1. contribute to our understanding of the onset of criminal behavior
2. general learning model has been criticized:
   a. fails to account for origin of criminal definitions
   b. implies that people systematically learn techniques that allow them to be active, successful criminals
   c. difficult to explain some criminal behaviors with this approach
3. important because they explain criminality across all class structures

III. Social control theory
1. maintains that all people have the potential to violate the law
2. asks why people obey the rules of society

A. Self-concept and crime
1. early research described delinquents as having weak egos and lacking self-control

B. Modern social control theory
1. version articulated by Hirschi is dominant
2. Hirschi links onset of criminality to the weakening of the ties that bind people to society
3. social bond can be divided into four main elements:
   a. attachment
   b. commitment
   c. involvement
   d. belief
4. the interrelationship of social bond elements controls subsequent behavior
5. Hirschi's data give support to the validity of social control theory
   a. others have corroborated research
6. other research has also raised questions concerning:
   a. friendship
   b. failure to achieve
   c. involvement and supervision

d. deviant peers and parents

IV. Social reaction (labeling) theory
    1. explains criminal careers in terms of destructive social interactions and stigma-producing encounters
    2. depending on the visibility of the label and the manner and severity with which it is applied, negatively labeled individuals will become increasingly committed to a deviant career

  A. Crime and labeling theory
    1. crime and deviance are defined by social audience reaction to people and their behavior and the effects of that reaction
    2. according to Becker, "deviant behavior is behavior that people so label"
    3. crime is viewed as a subjective concept
      a. definition depends on the viewing audience
    4. people who create rules are moral entrepreneurs

  B. Consequences of labeling
    1. negative labels stigmatize people and alter their self-image
    2. people who are labeled as deviant may join with other outcasts
    3. labels tend to redefine the whole person
    4. labels become the basis of personal identity

  C. Primary and secondary deviance
    1. concepts introduced by Lemert
    2. primary deviance involves norm violations or crimes that have little influence on the actor, are quickly forgotten
    3. secondary deviance occurs when deviant event comes to the attention of significant others or social control agents
      a. involves resocialization into a deviant role
      b. produces deviance amplification

  D. Research on social reaction theory
    1. can be classified into two distinct categories
      a. one focuses on the characteristics of the offender labeled
      b. one attempts to discover effects of being labeled
    2. evidence exists that poor and powerless are victimized by law and justice system
      a. labels are not equally distributed across class and racial lines
      a. the practice of contextual discrimination
    3. empirical evidence shows that negative label influences self-image
    4. empirical evidence supports view that labeling plays an important role in persistent offending

  E. Is labeling theory valid?
    1. important contributions to study of criminality:
      a. identifies the role played by social agents in crime causation
      b. recognizes that criminality is not a disease or pathological behavior
      c. distinguishes between primary and secondary deviance
      d. focuses on the interaction as well as the situation surrounding the crime

V. An evaluation of social process theory
    1. does not always account for some of the patterns and fluctuations in the crime rate
    2. leaves many questions unanswered

VI. Social process theory and social policy
    1. social process theories have had a major influence on social policies since the 1950s
    2. have greatly influenced the way criminal offenders are treated
    3. have influenced criminal justice and other social policies
    4. influence can be seen in diversion and restitution programs
    5. stigma-producing programs have not met with great success

VII. Summary

MULTIPLE CHOICE

1. Social process theories have endured because the relationship between _____ and crime is still uncertain.
    a. race
    b. family structure
    c. social class
    d. gender

2. Today, many criminologists discount the association between _____ and the onset of criminality.
    a. race
    b. family structure
    c. social class
    d. gender

3. Children as young as _____whose parents are drug abuses exhibit personality defects such as excessive anger and negativity.
    a. 2
    b. 3
    c. 4
    d. 5

4. Schools contribute to criminality by _____ problem youths, which set them apart from conventional society.
    a. expelling
    b. failing
    c. labeling
    d. ignoring

5. The social process approach has several independent branches. Which of the following is not one of these?
    a. social reaction theory
    b. social strain theory
    c. social control theory
    d. social learning theory

6. _____ theory suggests that people learn techniques and attitudes of crime from close relationships with criminal peers.
    a. Social reaction
    b. Social strain
    c. Social control
    d. Social learning

7. _____ theory says that people become criminals when significant members of society label them as such and they accept those labels as a personal identity.
    a. Social reaction
    b. Social strain
    c. Social control
    d. Social learning

8. _____ theories assume that people are born good and must learn to be bad.
    a. Social reaction
    b. Social strain
    c. Social control
    d. Social learning

9. _____theory assumes that whether good or bad, people are controlled by the evaluation of others.
   a. Social reaction
   b. Social strain
   c. Social control
   d. Social learning

10. One of the most prominent _____ theories is differential association theory.
   a. social reaction
   b. social strain
   c. social control
   d. social learning

11. Sutherland believed that acquiring a behavior is a _____ process.
   a. social reaction
   b. social strain
   c. social control
   d. social learning

12. People experience what Sutherland calls _____ when they are exposed to opposing attitudes toward right and wrong or moral and immoral.
   a. intensity
   b. culture conflict
   c. priority
   d. culture exposure

13. For Sutherland, _____ means the age of children when they first encounter definitions of criminality.
   a. intensity
   b. culture conflict
   c. priority
   d. culture exposure

14. Warr's research suggests that criminal peers are _____. One you get them, they are hard to lose.
   a. habit-forming
   b. "sticky"
   c. persistent
   d. "tough"

15. Sutherland's theory fails to account for the origin of
   a. learning.
   b. criminal behavior.
   c. criminal definitions.
   d. non-criminal behavior.

16. According to Matza and Sykes, learning _____ techniques allows a person to temporarily drift away from conventional behavior and become involved in antisocial behaviors.
   a. criminal
   b. neutralization
   c. conforming
   d. labeling

17. Young offenders sometimes claim that their unlawful acts are not their fault. This is an example of denial of
   a. injury.
   b. the victim.
   c. responsibility.
   d. higher loyalties.

18. Denial of the victim may help explain which type of crimes?
    a. property
    b. juvenile
    c. assault
    d. hate

19. Early versions of _____ theory speculated that criminality was a product of weak self-concept and poor self-esteem.
    a. control
    b. labeling
    c. learning
    d. strain

20. _____ theory explain criminal careers in terms of destructive social interactions and stigma-producing encounters.
    a. Control
    b. Labeling
    c. Learning
    d. Strain

TRUE/FALSE

1. According to labeling theory, depending on the visibility of the label and the manner and severity with which it is applied, negatively labeled individuals will become increasingly committed to a deviant career.

2. According to the social control approach, deviance is defined by the social audience's reaction to people and their behavior and the subsequent effects of that reaction.

3. In its purest form, social learning theory argues that even such crimes as murder, rape, and assault are only bad or evil because people label them as such.

4. Howard Becker refers to people who create rules as power mongrels.

5. A process known as retrospective reading means that the labeled person's past is reviewed and reevaluated to fit his or her current status.

6. One of the better-known views of the labeling process is Howard Becker's concept of primary and secondary deviance.

7. According to labeling theory, stigma helps lock people into a deviant career.

8. The branches of the social process theory are compatible because they all suggest that criminal behavior is part of the socialization process.

9. Learning theories have greatly influenced the way criminal offenders are treated.

10. The influence of control theory can be seen in diversion and restitution programs.

11. Social control theory analyzes the failure of society to control criminal tendencies.

12. Social reaction theory maintains that all people have the potential to become criminals.

13. Reckless suggests that a person's self-concept aids his or her commitment to conventional action.

14. Despite the importance of differential association theory, research devoted to testing its assumptions has been relatively sparse.

15. Control theory's focus on the family has played a key role in programs designed to strengthen the bond between parent and child.

FILL-IN REVIEW

1. Social learning theorists believe that crime is a product of learning the norms, values, and _____ associated with criminal activity.

2. One of the most prominent social learning theorists is _____.

3. _____ _____ theorists maintain that all people have the potential to violate the law and that modern society presents many opportunities for illegal activity.

4. According to Hirschi, without _____ _____, a person is free to commit criminal acts.

5. For Hirschi, _____ refers to a person's sensitivity to and interest in others.

6. According to Hirschi, social control is measured by a person's attachment, commitment, involvement, and _____.

7. Howard Becker refers to people who create rules as _____ _____.

8. A _____ _____ theorist views crime as a subjective concept whose definition depends entirely on the viewing audience.

9. A major premise of _____ _____ theory is that the law is differentially constructed and applied, depending on the offender.

10. According to Lemert, _____ deviance involves norm violations or crimes that have little influence on the actor and can be quickly forgotten.

11. Secondary deviance produces a _____ _____ effect.

12. _____ deviants view themselves as good people who have done a bad thing.

13. Social process theories have endured because the relationship between _____ _____ and _____ is still uncertain.

14. Differential association may vary in frequency, duration, priority, and _____.

15. Many criminologists consider _____ _____ theory the most important way of understanding the onset of youthful misbehavior.

ESSAY QUESTIONS

1. Discuss the basic concept of social learning theories, and then explain why these theories have endured.

2. What does the research tell us about family relationships as a major determinant of behavior?

3. Are learning theories valid? Explain why or why not.

4. Discuss what this research has shown about Hirschi's social control theory.

5. An important principle of social reaction theory is that the law is differentially applied. Discuss this.

CHAPTER 7 ANSWER SECTION

MULTIPLE CHOICE

1.	c
2.	b
3.	a
4.	c
5.	b
6.	a
7.	a
8.	d
9.	a
10.	d
11.	d
12.	b
13.	c
14.	b
15.	c
16.	b
17.	c
18.	d
19.	a
20.	b

TRUE/FALSE

1.	T
2.	F
3.	F
4.	F
5.	T
6.	F
7.	T
8.	T
9.	T
10.	F
11.	T
12.	F
13.	T
14.	T
15.	T

FILL-IN REVIEW

1.	behaviors
2.	Sutherland
3.	Social control
4.	social bonds
5.	attachment
6.	belief
7.	moral entrepreneurs
8.	social reaction
9.	social reaction
10.	primary
11.	deviance amplification
12.	Primary
13	social class, crime
14.	intensity
15.	social control

8   Conflict Theory: It's a Dog-Eat-Dog World

LEARNING OBJECTIVES

After covering the material in this chapter, you should understand:

1. what issues concern conflict theorists.

2. common objectives of conflict theory.

3. why law is an integral part of society.

4. what the conflict-oriented research has taught us.

5. the importance of the radical approach to criminology.

6. the fundamentals of Marxist criminology.

7. what is meant by the conflict definition of crime.

8. how instrumental Marxists view criminal law and the criminal justice system.

9. the relationships among crime, victims, the criminal, and the state from a Marxist perspective.

10. why the Marxist approach has been critiqued.

11. which recent forms of radical theory have emerged, including radical feminist theory, power-control theory, postmodern theory, and peacemaking theory.

12. the impact of social conflict theory on social policy.

KEYWORDS

social conflict theory
radical criminology
Marxist criminology
power
social reality of crime
surplus value
marginalization
instrumental Marxist
demystify
structural Marxist
left realism
preemptive deterrence
Marxist feminism
patriarchal
power–control theory
postmodernist
deconstructionist
semiotics
peacemaking
restorative justice
sentencing circle

CHAPTER OUTLINE

I. The conflict theory of crime
      1. came into criminological prominence during the 1960s
      2. common objectives in Chambliss and Seidman's writing:
          a. relationship between political and economic system and the way criminal justice is administered
          b. demonstrating how definitions of crime favor those who control the justice system
          c. analyzing the role of conflict in contemporary society
  A. Power relations
      1. crime is defined by those in power
      2. unequal distribution of power produces conflict
      3. African Americans more likely to perceive criminal injustice
  B. The social reality of crime
      1. theory introduced by Quinney
      2. criminal definitions represent interests of powerful in society
      3. law is not an abstract body of rules; it is an integral part of society
  C. Research on conflict theory
      1. social inequality forces people to commit some crimes
      2. class bias exists in the criminal justice system
      3. members of powerless, disenfranchised groups more likely to be punished
      4. criminal justice system is disinterested when victim is poor, black, and female

II. Radical criminology
      1. influenced by writings of Marx and Engles
      2. locus of the radical approach to criminology in U.S. was in California
      3. U.S. radicals were influenced by widespread social unrest during the late 1960s and early 1970s
      4. Marxists did not enjoy widespread approval at major universities
  A. Fundamentals of Marxist criminology
      1. Marxism is a critique of capitalism
      2. crime is viewed as a function of the capitalist mode of production
      3. state is an ally of the wealthy
      4. conflict definition of crime is used
          a. crime is a political concept
      5. the nature of a society controls the directions of its criminality
      6. criminality is a function of social and economic orientation
      7. general theme is the relationship between crime and the ownership and control of private property
          a. ownership and control is the principal basis of power in U.S. society
      8. surplus value is an important aspect of the capitalist economic system
      9. marginalism is a condition that occurs as more people are thrust outside the economic mainstream
  B. Instrumental Marxism
      1. criminal law and criminal justice system are instruments for controlling the powerless in society
      2. capitalist justice serves the powerful and the rich
      3. it is essential to demystify law and justice
  C. Structural Marxists
      1. disagree with view that relationship between law and capitalism is unidirectional
      2. law is designed to keep the capitalist system operating efficiently
  D. Research on Marxist criminology
      1. Marxists rarely use standard social science methodologies
      2. offended by empirical studies
      3. efforts to test its fundamental assumptions quantitatively have been undertaken

        4.   relationships among crime victims, the criminal, and the state:
           a.   crime and its control are a function of capitalism
           b.   justice system is biased against the working class
        5.   goals of historical analysis are to show how changes in criminal law correspond to development of the capitalist economy and investigate development of modern police agencies

    E.   Critique of Marxist Criminology
        1.   has been accused of being "hot air, heat, but no real light"
        2.   substance of Marxist thought has been criticized
        3.   unfairly neglect the capitalist system's efforts to regulate itself

III.   Emerging forms of social conflict theory
    A.   Left realism
        1.   troubled by emergence of a strict "law and order policy"
        2.   most often connected to the writings of Lean and Young
           a.   their approach resembles the relative deprivation approach
        3.   argues that crime victims in all classes need and deserve protection
        4.   preemptive deterrence is an approach to eliminate or reduce crime
        5.   criticized by radical thinkers
    B.   Radical feminist theory
        1.   views gender inequality as stemming from unequal power of men and women
        2.   gender differences can be traced to development of private property and male domination of laws of inheritance
        3.   patriarchy is supported by capitalists
        4.   criminal behavior patterns linked to gender conflict
        5.   focus on the social forces that shape women's lives and experiences to explain female criminality
        6.   exploitation triggers onset of female delinquent and deviant behavior
        7.   indict the justice system and its patriarchal hierarchy
    C.   Power control theory
        1.   uses gender differences to explain onset of criminality
        2.   delinquency rates are a function of two factors:
           a.   class position (power)
           b.   family functions (control)
        3.   theory has received a great deal of attention
        4.   empirical support found
    D.   Postmodern theory
        1.   postmodernists also known as deconstructionists
        2.   embrace semiotics as a method of understanding criminal behavior
           a.   the use of language elements as signs or symbols beyond their literal meaning
        3.   rely on semiotics to conduct research
        4.   assert that those in power can use their own language to define crime and law
    E.   Peacemaking criminology
        1.   main purpose of criminology is to promote a peaceful, just society
        2.   view efforts of the state to control and punish as encouraging crime
        3.   try to find humanist solutions to crime and other social problems
           a.   advocate polices such as mediation and conflict resolution, rather than prison

IV.   Social conflict theory and social policy
        1.   crime rates will be reduced if conflict and competition are reduced
        2.   restorative justice turns the justice system into a healing process
           a.   typically diverts cases away from the formal court process

V. Summary

MULTIPLE CHOICE

1. Conflict theory came into criminological prominence during the
    a. 1940s.
    b. 1960s.
    c. 1980s.
    d. year, 2000.

2. Chambliss and Seidman wrote the well-respected treatise
    a. *Race, Gender, and Political Power.*
    b. *Power and Social Control.*
    c. *It's a Dog-Eat-Dog World.*
    d. *Law, Order, and Power.*

3. _____ refers to the ability of persons and groups to determine and control the behavior of others and to shape public opinion to meet their personal interests.
    a. Power
    b. Social control
    c. Authority
    d. Lawmaking

4. Police routinely search, question, and detain African American males in an area if a violent crime has been described as "looking or sounding black"; this is called
    a. gender profiling.
    b. racial discrimination.
    c. gender discrimination.
    d. racial profiling.

5. Richard Quinney integrated beliefs about power, _____, and criminality into a theory he referred to as the social reality of crime.
    a. race
    b. society
    c. gender
    d. social class

6. According to Quinney, law violations can be viewed as political or even _____ acts.
    a. necessary
    b. terrorist
    c. quasi-revolutionary
    d. retaliation

7. Conflict theorists argue that crime rates seem strongly related to measures of _____ inequality.
    a. gender
    b. racial
    c. social
    d. religious

8. The unemployed, especially racial minorities, may be perceived as _____ who present a real threat to society and must be controlled or incapacitated.
    a. "hot shots"
    b. "social dynamite"
    c. "a keg ready to blow"
    d. dangerous

9. Research shows that African Americans are sent to prison on _____ charges 27 to 50 times the rate of European Americans.
   a. homicide
   b. rape
   c. assault
   d. drug

10. Racism and _____ pervade the U.S. justice system and shape crime rates.
    a. genderism
    b. discrimination
    c. classism
    d. prejudice

11. In 1968, a group of _____ sociologists formed the National Deviancy Conference.
    a. American
    b. British
    c. Canadian
    d. French

12. Those in power use the fear of _____ as a tool to maintain their control over society.
    a. incarceration.
    b. death
    c. crime
    d. blacks

13. From a radical perspective, to control crime and reduce criminality is to end the social conditions that promote
    a. crime.
    b. punishment.
    c. inequality.
    d. humanism.

14. The poor, according to the _____ view, may or may not commit more crimes than the rich, but they certainly are arrested and punished more often.
    a. structural Marxism
    b. instrumental
    c. radical
    d. realist

15. Instrumental Marxists consider it essential to demystify law and justice – that is, to unmask its
    a. racism.
    b. true purpose.
    c. makers.
    d. secrets.

16. To a _____, the law is designed to keep the capitalist system operating efficiently.
    a. instrumentalist
    b. structuralist
    c. radical
    d. realist

17. From a Marxist perspective, social trends are interpreted with regard to how _____ has affected human interaction.
    a. capitalism
    b. social change
    c. racism
    d. classism

18. Some radical scholars are troubled by the emergence of a strict "_____" philosophy, which has a s its centerpiece a policy of punishing juveniles severely in adult court.
    a. lock 'em up and throw away the key
    b. three strikes and you're out
    c. Book 'em, Dano
    d. law and order

19. Left realism has been criticized by radical thinkers as
    a. being unrealistic.
    b. encouraging classism.
    c. legitimizing the existing power structure.
    d. arguing that only the crime victims of the lower social class need and deserve protection.

20. Marxist feminists link criminal behavior patterns to the gender conflict created by the economic and social struggles common in _____ societies.
    a. preliterate
    b. industrial
    c. socialist
    d. postindustrial

TRUE/FALSE

1. Marxist feminists point out that women are denied access to male-dominated street crimes.

2. Messerschmidt argues that in every culture, males struggle to dominate women in order to prove their manliness. This is called "doing gender."

3. Hagan's view is that crime and delinquency rates are a function of two factors: law and order.

4. Hagan and his associates found that when fathers and mothers hold equally valued managerial positions, the similarity between the rates of their daughters' and sons' delinquency is minimal.

5. Richard Quinney has shifted his theoretical orientation from conflict theory to Marxism and now to peacemaking.

6. Karl Marx's extensive writings on the topic of crime greatly influenced the development of social conflict thinking.

7. Social conflict theory seeks to evaluate how criminal law is used as a mechanism for social control.

8. Marxists used the structuralist definition of crime.

9. It is clear that a single view or theory defines Marxists criminology today.

10. Instrumental Marxists see the state as the tool of capitalists.

11. Marxist criminologists often use the standard social science methodologies to test their views.

12. To a structuralist, the law is designed to keep the capitalist system operating efficiently.

13. Most mainstream criminologists agree wholeheartedly with the substance of Marxist thought.

14. The peacemaking movement has applied nonviolent methods through what is known as just deserts.

15. Restorative programs typically divert cases away from the formal court process.

FILL-IN REVIEW

1. _____ _____ theory seeks to evaluate how criminal law is used as a mechanism of social control.

2. The idea of the social _____ of crime is that those who hold power in society define those who oppose their values as criminals.

3. _____ and _____ pervade the U.S. justice system and shape crime rates according to the social conflict theory.

4. _____ criminology tries to explain how the workings of the capitalist system produces inequality and crime.

5. _____ Marxists believe that the legal system supports the owners at the expense of the workers.

6. _____ Marxists believe that he law is used to maintain the long-term interests of the capitalist system.

7. Marxist research is designed to show how capitalism creates large groups of people who have no choice but to turn to _____ for survival.

8. _____ _____ are concerned with patriarchy and the oppression of women. They link female criminality to gender inequality.

9. _____-_____ theory shows how family structure, women's economic status, and gender inequality interact to produce male/female differences in the crime rate.

10. _____ analyze how language is used to control thought and behavior.

11. _____ criminologists seek nonviolent, humane alternatives to coercive punishment.

12. At the core of all the various branches of social conflict theory is the premise that _____ causes crime.

13. _____ turns the justice system into a healing process rather than a distributor of retribution and revenge.

14. Marxist criminology views the competitive nature of the _____ _____ as a major cause of crime.

15. Deconstructionism looks at the symbolic meaning of _____ and culture.

ESSAY QUESTIONS

1. Discuss Hagan's power-control theory.

2. Discuss why, from the Marxist perspective, the relationship between power and conflict is evident in the racism that pervades the justice process.

3. Discuss why Marxists rarely use standard social science methodologies to test their views.

4. Discuss how the justice system penalizes women from the radical feminist point of view.

5. Discuss peacemaking criminology

CHAPTER 8 ANSWER SECTION

MULTIPLE CHOICE

1. b
2. d
3. a
4. d
5. b
6. c
7. c
8. b
9. d
10. c
11. b
12. c
13. a
14. b
15. b
16. b
17. a
18. d
19. c
20. d

TRUE/FALSE

1. T
2. T
3. F
4. F
5. T
6. F
7. T
8. F
9. F
10. T
11. F
12. T
13. F
14. F
15. T

FILL-IN REVIEW

1. Social conflict
2. reality
3. Racism, classism
4. Marxist
5. Instrumental
6. Structural
7. crime
8. Radical feminists
9. Power-control theory
10. Postmodernists
11. Peacemaking
12. conflict
13. Restoration
14. capitalist system
15. law

9 Integrated Theories: Things Change

LEARNING OBJECTIVES

After covering the material in this chapter, you should understand:

1. the ways in which latent trait theories and development theories view criminality.

2. the concept of latent traits model proposed by Rowe, Osgood, and Nicewander.

3. the basic assumptions and critiques of Gottfredson and Hirschi's general theory of crime.

4. Tittle's concept of control and its two elements.

5. the importance of the Glueck research.

6. concepts associated with the developmental perspective.

7. how the social developmental model integrates social control, social learning, and structural models.

8. why the interact ional theory sees the causes of crime as bi-directional.

9. how, according to age-graded theory, building social capital and strong social bonds reduces the likelihood of long-tem deviance.

KEYWORDS

integrated theory
developmental criminology
latent trait theory
developmental theory
latent trait
general theory of crime (GTC)
control balance theory
life-course theory
problem behavior syndrome (PBS)
authority conflict pathway
covert pathway
overt pathway
adolescent-limited
life-course persister
pseudomaturity
social development model (SDM)
prosocial bonds
interactional theory
turning points
social capital
coercion
interpersonal coercion
impersonal coercion

CHAPTER OUTLINE

I. Latent trait theories
    1. Rowe, Osgood, and Nicewander proposed concept of latent traits
        a. personal attribute or characteristic that controls inclination or propensity to commit crimes
        b. propensity to commit crime is stable; opportunity fluctuates
  A. General theory of crime
    1. developed by Gottfredson and Hirschi
    2. redefines some principles found in Hirschi's social control theory
    3. considers the criminal offender and the criminal act as separate concepts
    4. adds a biosocial element to concept of social control
    5. tendency to commit crimes related to person's level of self-control
        a. traces the roots of poor self-control to inadequate child-rearing practices
    6. claims to explain all varieties of criminal behavior, as well as correlates of crime
    7. some empirical support found
    8. critiques center around:
        a. tautological reasoning
        b. personality disorder
        c. ecological/individual differences
        d. racial and gender differences
        e. people change
        f. modest relationships
        g. cross-cultural differences
    9. strength of theory is in its scope and breadth
  B. Control balance theory
    1. expands on concept of personal control as predisposing element for criminality
    2. concept of control has two elements:
        a. amount of control one is subjected to by others
        b. amount of control one can exercise over others
    3. Tittle sees control as a continuous variable
    4. an excess of control can lead to deviance and crime
    5. this view is essentially integrated
        a. it incorporates external or social concepts with internal or individual variables

II. Developmental theory
    1. sometimes referred to as life-course theory
    2. recognizes that as people mature, factors that influence their behavior change
    3. inherently multidimensional
  A. The Glueck research
    1. focused on early onset of delinquency as a harbinger of a criminal career
    2. identified a number of personal and social factors related to persistent offending
    3. did not restrict analysis to social variables
  B. Developmental concepts
    1. view of crime that incorporates personal change and growth
        a. recognizes factors that produce crime and delinquency at one point in life-cycle may not be relevant at another
    2. problem behavior syndrome (PBS)
        a. crime is just one among a group of antisocial behaviors that cluster together
        b. those who exhibit PBS are prone to more difficulties than the general population
    3. three distinct paths to a criminal career:
        a. authority conflict pathway
        b. covert pathway
        c. overt pathway

4. a small group of life-course persisters offend well into adulthood
   a. pseudomaturity
5. continuity of crime
   a. best predictor of future criminality is past criminality
   b. criminal propensity may be "contagious"
6. strong support found for developmental theory

III. Theories of criminal development
   A. The social development model (SDM)
      1. different factors affect a child's social development over the life course
      2. children are socialized and develop bonds through four distinct interactions and processes:
         a. perceived opportunities for involvement with others
         b. degree of involvement and interaction with parents
         c. ability to participate in these interactions
         d. reinforcement they perceive for participation
      3. prosocial bonds control risk of antisocial behavior
   B. Interact ional theory
      1. an age-graded view of crime
      2. holds that seriously delinquent youths form belief systems that are consistent with their deviant lifestyles
      3. key idea is that causal influences are bi-directional
      4. Thornberry suggests that criminality is a developmental process
      5. suggests that criminality is part of a dynamic social process
   C. Sampson and Laub: age-graded theory
      1. identify turning points in a criminal career
      2. supported by research
      3. building social capital and strong social bonds reduces the likelihood of long-term deviance
      4. conducting follow-up to their original research
         a. findings suggest that delinquency and other forms of antisocial conduct in childhood related to adult crime and drug and alcohol abuse
      5. desistence related to "knifing off"
      6. prevention of crime must be a policy at all times and in all stages of life

IV. Summary

MULTIPLE CHOICE

1. ____ trace the root cause of poor self-control to inadequate child-rearing practices.
   a. Loeber and his associates
   b. The Glueks
   c. Sampson and Laub
   d. Gottfredson and Hirschi

2. ____ claimed that children who had a mesomorph physique were most likely to become persistent offenders.
   a. Loeber and his associates
   b. The Gluecks
   c. Sampson and Laub
   d. Gottfredson and Hirschi

3. The concept of latent traits was proposed by
   a. Rowe, Osgood, and Nicewander
   b. Tittle
   c. Thornberry
   d. Sampson and Laub

4. According to the general theory of crime, people who have ____ are crime-prone even if they are born into affluent families.
   a. a latent trait
   b. poor self-esteem
   c. low self-control
   d. PBS

5. According to the ____ model, children must develop prosocial bonds in order to control the risk of antisocial behavior.
   a. general theory of crime
   b. social development
   c. PBS
   d. age-graded

6. According to this view, the propensity to commit crime is stable, but the opportunity fluctuates over time.
   a. general theory of crime
   b. social development
   c. latent trait
   d. interactional

7. In this theory of crime, the criminal offender and the criminal acts are seen as separate concepts.
   a. general theory of crime
   b. social development model
   c. latent trait
   d. interactional

8. Gottfredson and Hirschi claim that the principles of ____ theory can explain all varieties of criminal behavior.
   a. latent trait
   b. self-esteem
   c. self-control
   d. PBS

9. If a theory is accused of involving circular reasoning, it is said to be ____

a. confusing.
b. tautological.
c. phenomenological.
d. Methodological

10. According to Tittle, the concept of control has _____ elements.
a. one
b. two
c. three
d. four

11. Developmental theories are sometimes referred to as
a. life-style theories
b. life-cycle theories
c. life-course theories
d. life-content theories.

12. Developmental theories are inherently
a. unidimensional.
b. bidimensional.
c. multidimensional.
d. None of the above.

13. The Glueks' research focused on
a. latent traits.
b. poor self-control.
c. social variables only.
d. early onset of delinquency as a harbinger of a criminal career.

14. Crime is just one among a group of antisocial behaviors that cluster together, referred to collectively as
a. problem behavior syndrome.
b. psychological behavior syndrome.
c. behavior syndrome.
d. antisocial behavior syndrome.

15. Which of the following is not one of the pathways to crime identified by Loeber and his associates?
a. overt pathway
b. covert pathway
c. peer pressure pathway
d. authority conflict pathway

16. Maturing faster and engaging in early sexuality and drug use is referred to as
a. psuedosexualmaturity.
b. pseudomaturity.
c. psuedosexuality.
d. pseudoadolescence.

17. Pioneering criminologists _____ tracked the onset and termination of criminal careers.
a. Sampson and Laub
b. Loeber and his associates.
c. Sheldon and Eleanor Gluek
d. Gottfredson and Hirschi

18. To control the risk of antisocial behavior, a child must maintain _____ bonds.
a. presocial
b. prosocial
c. latent

d. All of the above

19. Thornberry has proposed an age-graded view of crime that he calls _____ theory.
    a. latent
    b. social bond
    c. interactional
    d. social developmental

20. Sampson and Laub found that one important element for "going straight" was
    a. "knifing off."
    b. "scripting off."
    c. "cooling off."
    d. "turning off."

TRUE/FALSE

1. Integrated theories focus attention on the relationship between gender and delinquency.

2. Charles Tittle developed the general theory of crime.

3. According to the Glueks, children who have a mesomorph physique were most likely to become persistent offenders.

4. Gottfredson and Hirschi trace the root cause of poor self-control to inadequate child-rearing practices.

5. The social development model integrates social control, social learning, and biosocial models.

6. According to the general theory of crime, an impulsive personality is the key latent crime-producing trait.

7. According to the latent trait view, the propensity to commit crime is stable.

8. Gottfredson and Hirschi consider the criminal offender and the criminal act as the same concept.

9. Some critics of GTC argue that the theory is vague.

10. The Glueks identified family relations as the most important social factor related to persistent offending.

11. Gottfredson and Hirschi claim that the principles of self-control theory can explain violent crime only.

12. One explanation for future criminality suggest that criminal propensity may be contagious.

13. Mark Colvin has developed an integrated theory that he calls differential coercion theory.

14. According to the interactional theory, the causes of crime are multidimensional.

15. Developmental theories are inherently unidimensional.

FILL-IN REVIEW

1. Integrated theories seek to avoid the shortcomings of _____- _____ theories.

2. Integrated theories focus their attention on the _____ _____.

3. _____ theorists view criminality as a dynamic process influenced by individual characteristics as well as social experiences.

4. The _____ _____ model assumes that a number of people in the population have a personal attribute or characteristic that controls their inclination or propensity to commit crime.

5. By recognizing that there are stable differences in people's propensity to commit crime, the GTC adds a _____ element to the concept of social control.

6. Gottfredson and Hirschi claim that the principles of self-control theory can explain

_____ _____ _____ _____

_____.

7. Tittle's _____ _____ theory expands on the concept of personal control as a predisposing element of criminality.

8. _____ _____ theories assume that people have a physical or psychological trait that makes them crime-prone.

9. The _____ _____ pathway begins at an early age with stubborn behavior.

10. _____ theories look at such issues as the onset of crime, escalation of offenses, continuity of crime, and desistance from crime.

11. The concept of _____ _____ syndrome suggests that criminality may be just one of a cluster of social, psychological, and physical problems.

12. _____-_____ _____ exhibit early onset of crime and then persist into adulthood.

13. The social development model (SDM) integrates social control, social learning, and _____ models.

14. According to the _____-_____ theory, building social capital and strong social bonds reduces the likelihood of long-term deviance.

15. According to the interactional theory, the causes of crime are _____.

ESSAY QUESTIONS

1. Several indicators support the validity of age-graded theory. Discuss what the evidence tells us.

2. Using data from a longitudinal cohort study, Loeber and his associates have identified three distinct paths to a criminal career. Discuss each of these paths.

3. Your text states the Sheldon and Eleanor Gluek were pioneering criminologists. Explain why this is so.

4. Summarize the general theory of crime, and the discuss the criticisms of this theory.

5. Discuss the social developmental model (SDM). How does it explain criminal behavior?

CHAPTER 9 ANSWER SECTION

MULTIPLE CHOICE

1. d
2. b
3. a
4. c
5. b
6. c
7. a
8. a
9. b
10. b
11. d
12. c
13. d
14. a
15. d
16. d
17 c
18. b
19. c
20. a

TRUE/FALSE

1. F
2. F
3. T
4. T
5. F
6. T
7. T
8. F
9. F
10. T
11. F
12. T
13. T
14. T
15. F

FILL-IN REVIEW

1. single-factor
2. chronic offender
3. Developmental
4. latent traits
5. biosocial
6. all varieties of criminal behavior
7. control balance theory
8. Latent trait
9. authority conflict
10. Developmental
11. problem behavior syndrome
12. Life-course persisters
13. structural
14. age-graded
15. bi-directional

10 Violent Crime

LEARNING OBJECTIVES

After covering the material in this chapter, you should understand:

1. the competing explanations offered for the causes of violent behavior.

2. the concept of the subculture of violence.

3. how substance abuse influences violence.

4. the effect of guns on the severity of violence.

5. what the UCR tells us about the incidence of rape.

6. the link between the military and rape.

7. the differences between the types of rape discussed.

8. the explanations offered for the predisposal to commit rape.

9. the relationship between rape and the law.

10. the degrees and types of homicide discussed.

11. demographic and social factors associated with murder.

12 the nature and patterns of assault.

13. what the research tell us about robbery.

14. emerging categories of interpersonal violence such as stalking, carjacking, hate crimes, and workplace violence.

15. political violence in terms of terrorism, as well as the forms of terrorism discussed.

KEYWORDS

robbery
instrumental violence
expressive violence
subculture of violence
rape
gang rape
acquaintance rape
date rape
marital rape
marital exemption
statutory rape
shield laws
murder
malice
actual malice

constructive malice
first-degree murder
premeditation
deliberation
felony murder
second-degree murder
manslaughter
voluntary manslaughter
involuntary manslaughter
thrill killing
serial killer
mass murderer
battery
assault
aggravated assault
child abuse
sexual abuse
spouse abuse
stalking
carjacking
hate crime
terrorism
genocide

CHAPTER OUTLINE

I.   The roots of violence
    A.   Personal traits
        1.   murderous youth shows signs of neurological impairment
        2.   abnormal personality structures associated with spousal and family abuse
    B.   Ineffective families
        1.   research traces violence to rejecting, ineffective, or abusive parenting
        2.   abused children often later engage in delinquent behaviors
    C.   Evolutionary factors/human instinct
        1.   Freud believed human aggression and violence are produced by:
            a.   eros
            b.   thantos
    D.   Exposure to violence
        1.   exposure to violence may cause children to display violent behavior
        2.   exposure to violence may have an effect on adults, even police
    E.   Cultural values
        1.   interpersonal violence more common in large, urban, inner-city areas
        2.   disproportionately a subculture of violence
    F.   Substance abuse
        1.   linked to violence in three ways:
            a.   psychopharmacological relationship
            b.   economic compulsive behavior
            c.   systematic link
    G.   Firearm availability
        1.   firearms a facilitating factor in violence
        2.   evidence indicates that more than 80 percent of inmates in juvenile correctional facilities owned a gun just before their confinement

II.   Forcible rape
    A.   History of rape
        1.   recognized as a crime throughout history

2. common in early civilization
3. forcible sex outlawed in late fifteenth century if victim was of the nobility
    a. sixteenth century before married and peasant women considered victims of rape
B. Incidence of rape
1. about 89,000 rapes, or attempted rapes, reported to U.S. police in 1999
    a. rate is 64 per 100,000 females
2. population density influences rape
    a. metropolitan areas have higher rates than rural areas
3. police make arrests in about half of all reported rape offenses
4. racial pattern of rape fairly consistent for some time
5. rape is a warm weather crime
6. NCVS estimates that 201,000 rapes and attempted rapes took place in 1999
C. Rape and the military
1. rape has been long associated with military conquest
2. "rape ring" at Aberdeen Proving Grounds in Maryland
3. belief that women are part of the spoils of war continues
D. Types of rape
1. gang rapes involve multiple attackers, more likely to involve alcohol and drugs
2. acquaintance rapes include:
    a. date rape
    b. marital rape
3. Groth
    a. elements of rape encounter
    b. classified personalities of rapists
4. date rape believed to be frequent on college campuses
    a. 15 to 20 percent of all college women are victims of rape or attempted rape
    b. fewer than 1 in 10 date rapes reported to police
5. Rideout filed rape charges against her husband in 1978
6. marital exemption doctrine meant legally married husband could not be charged with raping his wife
    a. research indicates each year many women are raped by their husbands
    b. today, most states recognize marital rape as a crime
7. statutory rape refers to sexual relations between an underage minor female and an adult male
E. The causes of rape
1. evolutionary, biological aspects of the male sexual drive
    a. suggests that rape may be instinctual
2. rape is a function of modern male socialization
    a. boys taught to be aggressive, tough, forceful, and dominating
    b. "virility mystique"
3. men who hold macho attitudes more likely to engage in sexual violence
4. men learn to commit rapes much as they learn any other behavior
5. an association exists between age of rapists and their victims
F. Rape and the law
1. prosecution of rape has always been a problem
2. proving guilt in a rape case is challenging for prosecutors
3. rape laws have been changing around the country
    a. shield laws
    b. 1991, *Michigan v. Lucas*
        1. U.S. Supreme Court upheld validity of shield laws
4. Violence Against Women Act passed in 1994

III. Murder and homicide
1. murder is most serious of all common-law crimes
    a. can still be punished by death

2. actual malice – state of mind assumed to exist when murder committed
3. constructive malice – when death results from negligent or unthinking behavior

A. Degrees of murder
  1. three degrees:
    a. first-degree murder
      1. premeditation
      2. deliberation
    b. second-degree murder
      1. malice aforethought
    c. manslaughter
      1. voluntary manslaughter
      2. involuntary manslaughter
  2. issue of whether an unborn fetus can be a murder victim has received attention

B. The nature and extent of murder
  1. rate was 5.7 per 100,000 in 1999
  2. victims tend to be males over age 18
  3. African Americans more likely to commit murder and to become murder victims
  4. murder tends to be an interracial crime

C. Murderous relations
  1. acquaintance homicide
    a. significant gender differences in homicide trends among unmarried people
    b. females more likely to kill mate after repeated violent attacks
    c. men kill partners because they fear losing control and power
    d. some murders involve a love triangle
  2. stranger homicides usually occur in the aftermath of a common law crime
  3. types of stranger homicide:
    a. thrill killing
    b. serial murder
    c. mass murder

IV. Assault and battery
  1. two separate crimes
    a. battery requires offensive touching
    b. assault requires no actual touching, but attempted battery or intentionally frightening victim by word or deed
  2. felonies when a weapon is used or when they occur during commission of a felony

A. Nature and patterns of assault
  1. pattern is similar to homicide
  2. 1999 rate – 336 per 100,000 inhabitants
  3. offenders are usually young, male, and white
  4. assault victims tend to be male
  5. NCVS assault rates by gender:
    a. males – 32 per 100,000
    b. females – 24 per 100,000

B. Assault in the home
  1. child abuse
    a. child neglect
    b. sexual abuse
  2. spouse abuse
    a. married women at greater risk than single people who live together

V. Robbery
  1. 1999 rate – 150 per 100,000 population
  2. northeastern states have highest robbery rates
  3. most often a street crime

4. most robbers opportunistic
5. appears to peak during winter months

VI. Emerging forms of interpersonal violence
    A. Stalking
       1. affects about 1.4 million victims annually
       2. most victims know their stalkers
       3. stalkers induce fear, but do not always make overt threats against their victims
       4. usually stops within one to two years
    B. Carjacking
       1. legally considered a type of robbery
       2. accounts for about 2 percent of all car thefts per year
       3. carjackers are basically violent
       4. both victims and offenders tend to be young black men
    C. Hate crimes
1. directed toward a particular person or members of a group because of race or ethnicity, gender, or religion
       2. usually involve convenient, vulnerable targets
       3. three types of hate crimes:
           a. thrill-seeking
           b. reactive
           c. mission
       4. 1999, about 8,000 bias-motivated criminal incidents reported; involved 10,000 victims
    D. Workplace violence
       1. typical offender: middle-aged white male who faces termination
       2. more than 2 million U.S. residents become victims of violent crime while they work
           a. assault is most common type of victimization
       3. third parties used to mediate disputes before they escalate into violence

VII. Political violence
    A. Terrorism
       1. defined as a type of political crime
       2. distinguished from conventional warfare
    B. Forms of terrorism
       1. revolutionary terrorists
       2. political terrorists
       3. nationalist terrorism
       4. cause-based terrorism
       5. environmental terrorism
       6. state-sponsored terrorism
    C. Responses to terrorism
       1. law enforcement agencies have infiltrated terrorist groups
       2. rewards often offered for information leading to arrests of terrorists
       3. antiterrorist legislation
           a. Antiterrorism and Effective Death Penalty Act of 1996

VIII. Summary

MULTIPLE CHOICE

1. Psychologist Lewis and her associates found that murderous youths show signs of
   a. weak social bonds.
   b. major neurological impairment.
   c. the subculture of violence.
   d. all of the above.

2. Sigmund Freud believed that human aggression and violence are produced by two instinctual drives:
   a. ego and id
   b. eros and ethos
   c. super-ego and thanatos
   d. eros and thanatos

3. Wolfgang and Ferracuti attribute disproportionately high violence rates to a
   a. poor family background.
   b. subculture of violence.
   c. neurological impairment.
   d. weak social bond.

4. Drug testing shows that in some areas, almost _____ percent of all people arrested are also drug abusers.
   a. 25
   b. 50
   c. 75
   d. 99

5. In the U.S., about _____ of firearms used in crimes are stolen or obtained through illegal means.
   a. 20
   b. 40
   c. 60
   d. 80

6. Peasant women and married women were not considered rape victims until well into the _____ century.
   a. fourteenth
   b. fifteenth
   c. sixteenth
   d. seventeenth

7. It has been estimated that _____ percent of all college women are victims of rape or attempted rape.
   a. 10 to 12
   b. 15 to 20
   c. 25 to 30
   d. 40 to 50

8. Traditionally, a legally married husband could not be charged with raping his wife; this legal doctrine was referred to as the
   a. marital exemption.
   b. wife rape exemption.
   c. legal rape exemption
   d. spouse exemption.

9. The term _____ refers to sexual relations between an underage minor female and an adult male.
   a. date rape

b. forcible rape
c. statutory rape
d. felony rape

10. Most states and the federal government have developed _____ laws which protect women from being questioned about their sexual history unless it directly bears on the case.
    a. anonymity
    b. shield
    c. obscurity
    d. cover

11. In an important 1991 case, *Michigan v. Lucas*, the U.S. Supreme Court upheld the validity of _____ laws.
    a. anonymity
    b. shield
    c. obscurity
    d. cover

12. _____ is considered to exist when a death results from negligent or unthinking behavior.
    a. Actual malice
    b. Unconscious malice
    c. Threatened malice
    d. Constructive malice

13. _____ means the killing was planned after careful thought rather than carried out on impulse.
    a. Premeditation
    b. Deliberation
    c. Second-degree murder
    d. Manslaughter

14. This type of murder occurs when a person's wanton disregard for the victim's life and his or her desire to inflict serious bodily harm on the victim result in the victim's death.
    a. premeditation
    b. deliberation
    c. second-degree murder
    d. manslaughter

15. The pattern of criminal assault is similar to that of
    a. homicide.
    b. rape.
    c. robbery.
    d. spouse abuse.

16. Gottman found that batterers tend to fall into one of two categories. What are they?
    a. Bulls and Tigers
    b. Pit Bulls and Cobras
    c. Rats and Snakes
    d. Hitters and Slappers

17. Most robbers are
    a. professional.
    b. chronic offenders.
    c. opportunistic.
    d. alcoholics.

18. Stalking is a problem that affects _____ victims annually.

a. 1 million
b. 1.2 million
c. 1.3 million
d. 1.4 million

19. Legally, carjacking is considered a type of
    a. theft.
    b. robbery.
    c. assault.
    d. all of the above.

20. Which of the following is not one of the three types of hate crimes identified by McDevitt and Levin?
    a. thrill-seeking
    b. reactive
    c. revenge
    d. mission

TRUE/FALSE

1. Fewer than one in two rapes is reported to the police.

2. Victims of severe child abuse seldom become violence-prone adults.

3. Criminologists consider rape a forceful expression of sexuality.

4. Some researchers argue that rape is a function of modern male socialization.

5. Grath found that 40 percent of the rapists he studied had been sexually victimized as adolescents.

6. Only a few states have developed shield laws.

7. Manslaughter is usually punished by anywhere between 1 and 15 years in prison.

8. Second-degree murder occurs when a person kills another after premeditation and deliberation.

9. Murder tends to be an intraracial crime.

10. Acquaintance homicide is the most common form of murder.

11. Mass murderers kill over a long period of time.

12. There is little empirical evidence to suggest that blended families have been linked to abuse.

13. Southern states have by far the highest robbery rate, according to the UCR.

14. In most cases stalking continues for five years or more.

15. The most common type of workplace victimization is assault.

FILL-IN REVIEW

1. _____ terrorists use violence against a regime which they consider to have unjustly taken control of their land either by force or coercion.

2. _____ terrorism promotes the interests of a minority ethic or religions group that has been prosecuted under majority rule in an effort to secure a homeland within the country.

3. _____-_____terrorism occurs when a repressive government regime forces its citizens into obedience, oppresses minorities, and stifles political dissent.

4. More than _____people are the targets of hate crimes each year in the U.S.

5. Legally, _____ is considered a type of robbery.

6. _____ can be defined as a course of conduct directed at a specific person that involves repeated physical or visual proximity, nonconsensual communication, or verbal, written, or implied threats sufficient to cause fear in a reasonable person.

7. The pattern of assault is quite similar to that of _____.

8. _____ requires offensive touching, such as slapping, hitting, or punching a victim.

9. Homicide without malice is called _____.

10. The _____ _____ _____ Act (1994) allows rape victims to sue in federal court on grounds that sexual violence violates their civil rights.

11. Most states and the federal government have developed _____ laws, which protect women from being question about their sexual history unless it directly bears on the case.

12. The _____/_____ _____ perspective suggests that rape may be instinctual.

13. Most rape incidents occur during the months of _____and _____

14. Crimes that vent rage, anger, or frustration are known as _____ _____.

15. Disturbing evidence indicates that more than _____ percent of inmates in juvenile correctional facilities owned a gun just before their confinement.

ESSAY QUESTIONS

1. Discuss the different levels or degrees of homicide discussed in your text.

2. Discuss the male socialization and the hypermasculinity views of rape.

3. One issue that has received national attention is whether a murder victim can be an unborn fetus. What does your text tell us about this issue?

4. Your text discusses two forms of assault that occur within the home. Discuss what the research tells us about each of these types of assault.

5. Discuss the responses to terrorism discussed in your text.

CHAPTER 10 ANSWER SECTION

MULTIPLE CHOICE

1. b
2. d
3. b
4. c
5. d
6. c
7. b
8. a
9. c
10. b
11. b
12. d
13. b
14. c
15. a
16. b
17. c
18. d
19. b
20. c

TRUE/FALSE

1. T
2. F
3. F
4. T
5. T
6. F
7. T
8. F
9. T
10. T
11. T
12. F
13. F
14. F
15. T

FILL-IN REVIEW

1. Revolutionary
2. Nationalist
3. State-sponsored
4. 10,000
5. carjacking
6. Stalking
7. Homicide
8. Battery
9. manslaughter
10. Violence Against Women
11. shield
12. evolutionary/biological factors
13. July, August
14. expressive violence
15. 80

11   *Property Crimes*

LEARNING OBJECTIVES

After covering the material in this chapter, you should understand:

1. that theft is not unique to modern times.

2. the differences between occasional criminals and professional criminals.

3. the definition of larceny/theft.

4. the history of larceny/theft, including the concept of constructive possession.

5. the differences between petit larceny and grand larceny.

6. common forms of larceny theft: shoplifting, bad check writing, credit card theft, auto theft, fraud, confidence games, and embezzlement.

7. merchant privilege laws, target removal strategies, and target hardening strategies.

8. the differences between naïve check forgers and systematic forgers.

9. the various types of auto theft discussed.

10. measures taken to combat auto theft.

11. the definition of burglary and the nature and extent of this crime.

12. types of burglaries and types of burglars.

13. the definition of arson.

KEYWORDS

occasional criminal
situational inducement
professional criminal
larceny
constructive possession
petit (petty) larceny
grand larceny
shoplifting
booster
fence
snitch
merchant privilege laws
target removal strategy
target hardening strategy
naive check forgers
systematic forgers
false pretenses

fraud
confidence game
embezzlement
burglary
arson

CHAPTER OUTLINE

I.   History of theft
  1. theft is not unique to modern times
  2. three separate groups of property criminals were active in the eighteenth century
       a. skilled thieves
       b. smugglers
       c. poachers
II.   Contempory thieves
  1. occasional criminals
       a. occasional criminals do not define themselve by a criminalal role
       b. occasional property crime occurs when there is a situational inducement
  2. professional criminals
       a. professional thieves make significant income from their crimes
       b. numbers are relative few
III. Larceny theft
  1. one of the earliest common-law crimes created by English judges
       a. concept of constructive possession is a legal fiction
  2. petit (petty) larceny involves small amounts of money; is a misdemeanor
  3. grand larceny is a felony punished by a sentence in the state prison
  4. the most common of all crimes
  A. Shoplifting
  1. common form of larceny/theft
  2. incidents of shoplifting have increased greatly in past 20 years
  3. Cameron's study of shoplifters done in 1960s
       a. 10 percent of shoplifters were professionals
       b. boosters are professional shoplifters
       c. fences are people who buy stolen property
       d. snitches are amateur pilfers
  4. criminologists view shoplifters as people likely to reform if apprehended
  5. fewer than 10 percent of shoplifting incidents are detected
  6. merchant privilege laws are designed to protect retailers and their employees from lawsuits regarding improper or false arrests
  7. strategies to reduce or eliminate shoplifting
       a. target removal strategies
       b. target hardening strategies
  B. Bad checks
  1. Lemert identified two types of check forgers
       a. naïve check forgers – amateurs who do not believe their actions will hurt anyone
       b. systematic check forgers – make a substantial living by passing bad checks
  C. Credit card theft
  1. has become a major problem in the U.S.
  2. problem is compounded by thieves who set up bogus Internet sites
  3. problem is growing rapidly
  D. Auto theft
  1. another common larceny offense
  2. treated as a separate category in the UCR because of its frequency and seriousness
  3. type of auto theft
       a. joyriding

    b. short-term transportation
    c. long-term transportation
    d. profit
    e. commission of another crime
   4. efforts to combat auto theft
    a. study found that most car theft prevention methods have little effect on theft rates
  E. False pretenses/fraud
   1. involves misrepresenting a fact to gain property
   2. differs from traditional larceny
  F. Confidence games
   1. run by swindlers who separate victim from his/her money
   2. have gone high-tech
  G. Embezzlement
   1. first codified into law by English Parliament during sixteenth century
   2. impossible to know how many incidents occur annually
   3. has increased in the past two decades

IV. Burglary
   1. considered a more serious crime than larceny/theft
   2. forced entry is not a necessity in most states for the crime to occur
  A. The nature and extent of burglary
   1. three subclasses
    a. forcible entry
    b. unlawful entry (no force used)
    c. unlawful entry (force used)
   2. burglary rate has dropped 22 percent since 1995
   3. NCVS reports about 3.6 million burglaries either completed or attempted in 1999
  B. Types of burglaries
   1. most burglars motivated by need for cash in order to get high
   2. burglars approach their job in a rational, business-like manner
   3. some burglars strike the same victim more than once
  C. Careers in burglary
   1. Shover characterizes the "good burglar"
    a. technical competence
    b. personal integrity
    c. specialization in burglary
    d. financial success
    e. ability to avoid prison sentences
   2. Shover identified four key requirements of the trade
    a. learn the many skills needed to commit lucrative burglaries
    b. team up to form a criminal gang
    c. have inside information
    d. cultivate fences or buyers for stolen wares
V. Arson
   1. willful, malicious burning of a home, public building, vehicle, or commercial building
   2. several motives for arson include
    a. adults may be motivated by severe emotional turmoil
    b. some arsonists experience sexual pleasure from their crime
    c. people hire arsonists because they want to collect insurance money
    d. concealment of a crime
   3. juveniles are the most prolific fire starters

VI. Summary

MULTIPLE CHOICE

1. The Crusades of the _____ century inspired peasants and downtrodden noblemen to leave the shelter of their estates to prey upon passing pilgrims.
    a. 10th
    b. 11th
    c. 12th
    d. 13th

2. What famous thief gave himself the title of "Thief Taker General of Great Britain and Ireland?"
    a. Robin Hood
    b. Friar Tuck
    c. James Stewart
    d. Jack Wild

3. Criminologists suspect that most _____ crimes are the work of amateur occasional criminals, whose decision to steal is spontaneous and whose acts are unskilled, unplanned, and haphazard.
    a. economic
    b. violent
    c. property
    d. organized

4. Professional theft traditionally refers to _____ forms of criminal behavior that are undertaken with a high degree of skill for monetary gain and that maximize financial opportunities and minimize the possibilities of apprehension.
    a. violent
    b. organized
    c. nonviolent
    d. disorganized

5. As originally construed, larceny involved taking property that was in the possession of the
    a. king.
    b. church.
    c. rightful owner.
    d. person who had the property.

6. The original definition of larceny did not include crimes in which the thief had taken the property by
    a. force.
    b. deceit.
    c. accident.
    d. theft.

7. Most U.S. state criminal codes separate larceny into _____ categories.
    a. two
    b. three
    c. four
    d. five

8. Larceny/theft is probably the most _____ of all crimes.
    a. violent
    b. dangerous
    c. reported
    d. common

9. Professional shoplifters are sometimes called
    a. fences.

     b. snitches.

     c. heisters.

     d. boosters.

10. _____ laws are designed to protect retailers and their employees from lawsuits stemming from improper or false arrest of suspected shoplifters.

     a. Target removal

     b. Merchant privilege

     c. Target hardening

     d. Fugitive apprehension

11. _____ conducted the best-known study of check forgers more than 40 years ago.

     a. Mary Owen Cameron

     b. Richard Wright

     c. Neal Shover

     d. Edwin Lemert

12. _____ is one of the most highly reported or all major crimes.

     a. Arson

     b. Shoplifting

     c. Auto theft

     d. Burglary

13. _____ percent of all auto thefts are reported to the police.

     a. 25

     b. 50

     c. 75

     d. 98

14. The _____ system installs a hidden tracking device in cars: the device gives of a signal enabling the police to pinpoint its location.

     a. Hijack

     b. Lojcack

     c. Carjack

     d. Noisejack

15. In one scam, a Las Vegas-based telephone con game used the name _____ to defraud people out of more than $1.3 million by soliciting donations for various causes, including families of those killed in the Oklahoma City bombing.

     a. Victim Care Inc.

     b. Children of America, Inc.

     c. Feed America, Inc.

     d. Helping Hands, Inc.

16. Most U.S. courts require a serious breach of trust before a person can be convicted of

     a. false pretenses.

     b. embezzlement.

     c. confidence games.

     d. shoplifting.

17. A majority of states have removed the _____ element from burglary definitions.

     a. nighttime

     b. entry

     c. threat

     d. attack

18. In an important book called _____, Wright and Decker describe the working conditions of active burglars.
    a. *How to Catch a Thief*
    b. *The Way It's Done*
    c. *Con-Man at Work*
    d. *Burglars on the Job*

19. According to Shover, characteristics of the "good burglar" include all but which of the following?
    a. technical competence
    b. personal integrity
    c. specialization in burglary
    d financial need

20. Your text tells us that juveniles are arrested for a greater share of this crime than any other.
    a. arson
    b. auto theft
    c. shoplifting
    d. burglary

TRUE/FALSE

1. Juveniles are the most prolific fire starters.

2. The crime of false pretenses is the same as the crime of larceny.

3. Occasional criminals view themselves as committed career criminals.

4. Contemporary definitions of larceny include theft offenses that do not involve using force or threats on the victim.

5. The concept of constructive possession is a legal fiction.

6. Petit larceny is punished as a felony.

7. Criminologists view shoplifters as people who are not likely to reform even if apprehended and punished.

8. Locking goods into place is an example of a target hardening strategy.

9. Cashing bad checks to obtain money or property is a form of larceny.

10. 75 percent of all auto thefts are reported to police.

11. Burglary is not considered to be a much more serious crime than larceny theft.

12. Overall, the average loss for a burglary in 1999 was about $1,500 per victim.

13. Cromwell, Olson, and Avary found that many burglars had serious alcohol problems and that their criminal activity was, in part, aimed at supporting their alcohol abuse.

14. Arson is an older man's crime.

15. The crime of theft is unique to modern times.

FILL-IN REVIEW

1. _____ thieves are opportunistic amateurs who steal because of situation inducements.

2. _____ is the taking and carrying away of the constructive possession of another.

3. Passing bad checks without adequate funds is a form of _____.

4. Auto theft adds up to more than $_____ billion per year.

5. _____ occurs when trusted persons or employees take someone else's property for their own use.

6. _____ is the breaking and entering of a structure in order to commit a felony, typically a theft.

7. _____ burglars have careers in which they learn the tricks of the trade form older, more experienced pros.

8. _____ is the willful, malicious burning of a home, public building, vehicle, or commercial building.

9. _____ _____ defines the crime of burglary as "the breaking and entering of a dwelling house of another in the nighttime with the intent to commit a felony within."

10. To encourage the arrest of shoplifters, a number of states have passed _____ _____ laws.

11. _____ was one of the earliest common-law crimes created by English judges to define acts in which one person took for his or her own use the property of another.

12. _____ larceny is a felony punished by a sentence in the state prison.

13. People who buy stolen property, usually at half the original price, are called _____.

14. Lemert referred to amateur check forgers as _____ check forgers.

15. The crime of _____ involves misrepresenting a fact in a way that causes a victim to willingly give his or her property to the wrongdoer, who then keeps it.

ESSAY QUESTIONS

1. Discuss Mary Owen Cameron's research on shoplifters.

2. Edwin Lemert conducted the best-known study of check forgers more than 40 years ago. Discuss his findings.

3. Discuss the crime of embezzlement. How prevalent is it?

4. The legal definition of burglary has undergone considerable change since it common-law origins. Discuss these changes.

5. Discuss the nature and extent of burglary.

CHAPTER 11 ANSWER SECTION

MULTIPLE CHOICE

1. b
2. d
3. a
4. c
5. c
6. b
7. a
8. d
9. d
10. b
11. d
12. c
13. c
14. b
15. c
16. b
17. a
18. d
19. d
20. a

TRUE/FALSE

1. T
2. F
3. F
4. T
5. T
6. F
7. F
8. T
9. T
10. T
11. F
12. T
13. F
14. F
15. F

FILL-IN REVIEW

1. Occasional
2. Larceny
3. larceny
4. 7
5. Embezzlement
6. Burglary
7. Professional
8. Arson
9. Common law
10. merchant privilege
11. Theft (or Larceny)
12. Grand
13. fences
14. naïve
15. fraud (or false pretenses)

12 White-Collar and Organized Crime

LEARNING OBJECTIVES

After covering the material in this chapter, you should understand:

1. the definitions of white-collar and organized crime.

2. the similarities between white-collar crime and organized crime.

3. the nature of white-collar crime as a criminal phenomenon which is not unique to the U.S.

4. Moore's typology of the elements of organized crime: stings and swindles, chiseling, individual exploitation of institutional position, influence peddling and bribery, embezzlement and employee fraud, client fraud, corporate crime, and high-tech crime.

5. efforts taken to control Internet crime, as well as computer crime.

6. common techniques of computer crime such as the Trojan horse, the salami slice, super-zapping, the logic bomb, impersonation, and data leakage.

7. the explanations put forth to explain white-collar crime as presented in the text.

8. the various compliance and deterrence strategies taken by law enforcement.

9. the general traits of organized crime.

10. what types of activities are engaged in by organized criminals.

11. measures taken by federal and state governments to combat organized crime.

KEYWORDS

white-collar crime
organized crime
enterprise
corporate crime
chiseling
churning
front running
bucketing
insider trading
pilferage
bank fraud
passive neglect
affirmative tax evasion
organizational crime
restraint of trade
group boycott
price-fixing
virus
corporate culture view
self-control view

compliance strategies
deterrence strategies
Mafia
alien conspiracy theory
La Cosa Nostra
Racketeer Influenced and Corrupt Organization Act (RICO)

CHAPTER OUTLINE

I.   The nature of white-collar crime
          1.   phrase "white-collar crime" first used by Edwin Sutherland
                a. described criminal activities of the rich and powerful in the late 1930s
          2.   Sutherland's work considered a milestone in criminological history
                a. focus was on corporate criminality
                b. contemporary definitions of white-collar crime typically much broader
          3.   difficult to estimate extent and influence of white-collar crime on victims
          4.   white-collar crime not a uniquely U.S. phenomenon

II.   Components of white-collar crime
      A.   Stings and swindles
          1.   involves stealing through deception by individuals
                a.   institutional or business position used to bilk people out of money
          2.   white-collar swindlers usually charged with common-law crimes such as embezzlement or fraud
          3.   swindlers using fake religious identities bilk thousands of people out of $100 million per year
      B.   Chiseling
          1.   regularly cheating an organization, its consumers or both
                a.   charging for bogus auto repairs
                b.   cheating customers on home repairs
                c.   short-weighing
                d.   illegal use of information about company policies that have not been disclosed to public
          1.   pharmacists and lawyers have come under fire for unscrupulous behavior
          2.   chiseling takes place on the commodity and stock markets
                a.   insider trading is an example of this kind of chiseling
      C.   Individual exploitation of institutional position
          1.   individuals exploit their power or position in an organization by extorting money from people by threatening to withhold services victim has a right to expect
          2.   purchasing agents in large companies often demand a piece of the action for awarding contracts to suppliers and distributors
      D.   Influence peddling and bribery
          1.   individuals holding important institutional positions will sell power, influence, and information to outsiders
          2.   the victim is the person forced to pay for services he/she deserves
          3.   the victim of influence peddling is the organization compromised by its employees for their own interests
          4.   it has become common for legislators and other state officials to be forced to resign or even jailed for accepting bribes
          5.   agents of the criminal justice system have also gotten caught up in official corruption
          6.   police officers have been vulnerable to charges of corruption
                a. Knapp Commission
                b. Mollen Commission
          7.   passage of the Foreign Corrupt Practices (FCPA) in 1977

E. Embezzlement and employee fraud
   1. involves individuals' use of their positions to embezzle company funds or appropriate company property for themselves
   2. blue-collar employees have been involved in systematic theft of company property, commonly called pilferage
   3. management-level fraud is also quite common
F. Client fraud
   1. theft from an organization that advances credit to its clients or reimburses them for services rendered
   2. physicians have been caught cheating the federal government out of Medicare or Medicaid payments
   3. large health care providers have been accused of routinely violating the law in order to obtain millions of illegal payments
   4. bank fraud encompasses such diverse schemes as check kiting
   5. passive neglect (such as not paying taxes) is a misdemeanor
   6. affirmative tax evasion (such as covering up sources of income) is a felony
G. Corporate crime
   1. socially injurious acts committed by people who control companies to further their business interests
   2. for a corporation to be held criminally liable, the employee committing the crime must be acting within the scope of his or her employment and must have actual or apparent authority to engage in the particular act in question
   3. acts include price-fixing and illegal restraint of trade, false advertising, and use of company practices that violate environmental protection statutes
   4. restraint of trade involves a contract or conspiracy to stifle competition, create a monopoly, artificially maintain prices, or otherwise interfere with free market competition
   5. four types of market conditions so anticompetitive they are declared illegal through the Sherman Antitrust Act:
      a. division of markets
      b. the trying arrangement
      c. group boycotts
      d. price-fixing
   6. examples of corporate fraud
      a. deceptive pricing
      b. false claims and advertising
   7. environmental crimes fall under this category
      a. many workers are victims of this type of crime
      b. control of workers' safety has been the province of the Occupational Safety and Health Administration (OSHA)
H. High-tech crime
   1. high-tech crimes are a new breed of white-collar offenses
      a. Internet crimes
      b. computer crimes
   2. enforcement of laws relating to the Internet can fall to a number of different agencies
      a. Federal Trade Commission
      b. Secret Service
      c. State attorneys
   3. computer-related thefts are a new trend in employee theft and embezzlement
      a. The Trojan horse
      b. The salami slice
      c. "super-zapping"
      d. the logic bomb
      e. impersonation
      f. data leakage
   4. installing a virus in a computer system is a computer crime

5. Congress enacted the Counterfeit Active Device and Computer Fraud and Abuse Act (amended in 1986)
    a. In 1994, the Computer Abuse act was passed to update federal enforcement efforts
6. people who illegally copy software violate the Criminal Copyright Infringement Act

III.   The causes of white-collar crime
    1. there are probably as many explanations for white-collar crime as there are white-collar crimes
    2. formal theories of white-collar crime
        a. corporate culture view is that some business organizations promote white-collar criminality in the same way that lower-class culture encourages the development of juvenile gangs and street crime
        b. according to the self-control view, the motives that produce white-collar crimes are the same as those that produce any other criminal behavior, low self-control

IV.   Controlling white-collar crime
    1. on the federal level, detection of white-collar crime is primarily in the hands of administrative departments and agencies
    2. FBI has made enforcement of white-collar criminal law one of its three top priorities
    A.   Compliance strategies
        1. aim for law conformity without the necessity of detecting, processing, or penalizing individual violators
            a. set up administrative agencies to oversee business activity
            b. approach has been used to control environmental crimes
            c. avoid stigmatizing and shaming businesspeople by focusing on the act, rather than the actor, in white-collar crime
    B.   Deterrence strategies
        1. involve detecting criminal violations, determining who is responsible, and penalizing the offenders to deter future violations
            a. oriented toward apprehending violators and punishing them rather than creating conditions that induce conformity
            b. should work – and they have – because white-collar crime is a rational act whose perpetrators are extremely sensitive to the threat of criminal sanctions
            c. federal agencies have traditionally been reluctant to throw corporate executives in jail
            d. deterrence strategies have become increasingly common

V.   Organized crime
    A.   Characteristics of organized crime
        1. conspiratorial activity
        2. economic gain as primary goal
        3. activities not limited to providing illicit services
        4. employs predatory tactics
        5. conspiratorial groups are quick and effective in controlling and disciplining members
        6. organized crime is not synonymous with the Mafia
        7. does not include terrorists dedicated to political change
    B.   Activities of organized crime
        1. traditional sources of income are providing illicit materials and using force to enter into and maximize profits in legitimate businesses
            a. most income comes from narcotics distribution
            b. billions come from gambling, theft rings, and other illegal enterprises
            c. organized criminals have infiltrated labor unions and control pensions

C. The concept of organized crime
  1. alien conspiracy theory
      a. Mafia is centrally coordinated by national committee
      b. organized crime is made up of a national syndicate of 25+ Italian-dominated families called LaCosa Nostra
  2. not all criminologists believe in alien conspiracy theory
      a. see organized crime as a group of ethnically diverse gangs who compete for profit in the sale of illegal goods and services or use force and violence to extort money from legitimate enterprises
  3. enterprise syndicates
      a. involved in providing services: madams, drug distributors, bookmakers
  4. power syndicates
      a. perform no set task except to extort or terrorize
  5. many different ethnic groups operate in U.S. today
D. Controlling organized crime
  1. measures aimed at controlling organized crime
      a. Interstate and Foreign Travel or Transportation in Aid of Racketeering Enterprise Act (Travel Act)
          1. prohibits travel in interstate commerce or use of interstate facilities to promote, manage, establish, carry on, or facilitate unlawful activity
      b. Racketeer Influenced and Corrupt Organization Act (RICO)
          1. created new categories of offenses in racketeering activity
          2. included both state-defined crimes and federally defined crimes
          3. designed to limit patterns of organized criminal activity
      c. Strike Force Program
          1. operates in 18 cities
          2. brings together various state and federal law enforcement officers and prosecutors to work as a team against racketeering
E. The future of organized crime
  1. traditional organized crime syndicates are in decline
      a. reigning family heads are quite old; called the "Geritol gang"
      b. younger members lack the skill and leadership of older bosses
      c. membership is about half what it was 20 years ago
      d. many ranking leaders in prison
  2. the Mafia has been hurt by changing values in the U.S.
      a. white-ethnic inner-city neighborhoods have been shrinking
      b. Mafia has lost their political and social base of operations
      c. Code of silence is broken regularly

VI. Summary

MULTIPLE CHOICE

1. In the late 1930s, _____ used the phrase "white-collar crime" to describe the criminal activities of the rich and powerful.
   a. Mark Moore
   b. Edwin Sutherland
   c. Robert K. Merton
   d. Emile Durkheim

2. In _____, corruption by public officials accounts for a high percentage of all cases of economic crime, despite the fact that the penalty for corruption is death.
   a. Japan
   b. Russia
   c. the U.S.
   d. China

3. White-collar crime and organized crime are linked together because they involve
   a. criminals.
   b. businesses.
   c. entrepreneurship.
   d. money.

4. The collapse of the Bank of Credit and Commerce International is an example of which type of white-collar crime?
   a. corporate crime.
   b. client fraud
   c. chiseling
   d. stings and swindles

5. Charging for bogus auto repairs is an example of which type of white-collar crime?
   a. corporate crime.
   b. client fraud
   c. chiseling
   d. stings and swindles

6. Which of the following is not an example of securities fraud?
   a. churning
   b. front running
   c. scorching
   d. bucketing

7. Thirty years ago, New York Mayor John Linsay appointed a commission to investigate allegations of _____ corruption.
   a. attorney
   b. police
   c. union
   d. stock market

8. The police officer code of secrecy is referred to as the
   a. "blue curtain."
   b. code of Omerta.
   c. "wall of silence."
   d. "oath of the blue."

9. A car dealer would commit _____ by securing loans on titles to cars it no longer owned.
   a. tax evasion

110

b. embezzlement

c. chiseling

d. bank fraud

10. Your text discussed two types of tax fraud. They are passive neglect and
    a. active tax evasion.
    b. affirmative tax evasion.
    c. aggressive tax evasion.
    d. positive tax evasion.

11. The control of restraint of trade violation has its legal basis in the _____ Act.
    a. Sherman Antitrust
    b. Trade Violations
    c. Conspiracy
    d. RICO

12. _____ occurs when contractors provide the government or other corporations with incomplete or misleading information on how much it will actually cost to fulfill the contract they are bidding on or use mischarges once the contracts are signed.
    a. False claims
    b. Chiseling
    c. Deceptive pricing
    d. Fraud

13. The _____ Act punishes the knowing or negligent discharge of a pollutant into navigable waters.
    a. Clean Water
    b. Rivers and Harbors
    c. Streams and Lake
    d. Water Recovery

14. In a 1995 case, a Minnesota woman advertised the health benefits of "germanium" on an Internet provider, claiming that they cure AIDS, cancer, and other diseases. Germanium products have been banned because they cause irreversible _____ damage.
    a. heart
    b. kidney
    c. eye
    d. lung

15. If a computer is used to reprogram another for illicit purposes, this is an example of which type of computer crime?
    a. the Trojan horse
    b. the salami slice
    c. "super-zapping"
    d. the logic bomb

16. A _____ is a program that disrupts or destroys existing programs and networks.
    a. glitch
    b. virus
    c. germ
    d. zapper

17. People who illegally copy software violate which Act?
    a. Computer Illegality Act
    b. Computer Decency Act
    c. Computer Copyright Infringement Act
    d. Illegal Copying Act

18. Which of the following is not one of the five New York organized crime families?
    a. Gambino
    b. Gotti
    c. Columbo
    d. Bonnano

19. Chicago contains a single mob organization called the
    a. firm
    b. organization
    c. outfit
    d. syndicate

20. Some experts believe that _____ crime families, thanks to their control of gasoline terminals and distributorships in the New York metropolitan area, evade as much as $5 billion a year in state and federal taxes.
    a. Puerto Rican
    b. Japanese
    c. Chinese
    d. Russian

TRUE/FALSE

1. There is evidence to suggest that the Russian organized crime groups have cooperated with Mafia families in narcotics trafficking.

2. Indications exists that the traditional organized crime syndicates are on the increase.

3. A number of the reigning organized crime family "godfathers" are quite old, prompting some law enforcement officials to dub them the "over the hill gang."

4. Regularly cheating an organization, its consumers, or both is considered to be chiseling.

5. Bucketing refers to skimming customer trading profits by falsifying trade information.

6. The 1993 Mollen Commission was successful in eliminating police corruption in New York City.

7. Pilferage refers to the systematic theft of company property by blue-collar employees.

8. Passive neglect, or not paying taxes, is a misdemeanor.

9. The Rivers and Harbors Act of 1899 punishes any discharge of waste materials that damages natural water quality.

10. Another name for the Toxic Substance Control act is the "Superfund."

11. Use of data in a computer system for personal gain is a computer crime.

12. According to the corporate culture view, the motives that produce white-collar crimes are the same as those that produce any other criminal behaviors.

13. Compliance strategies aim for law conformity without the necessity of detecting, processing, or penalizing individual violators.

14. Organized crime has power and status as its primary goals.

15. Chicago contains a single mob organization called the Mafia.

FILL-IN REVIEW

1. _____-_____ crime involves illegal activities of people and institutions whose acknowledged purpose is profit through legitimate business transactions.

2. Price-fixing is a type of white-collar crime known as _____ crime.

3. _____ crime involves the illegal distribution of illegal material.

4. The Federal Water Pollution Act is more commonly called the _____ _____ Act.

5. If one computer is used to reprogram another for illicit purposes, the theft style is referred to as the _____ _____.

6. An employee sets up a dummy account in the company's computerized records; the theft style is referred to as the _____ _____.

7. A _____ is a program that disrupts or destroys existing programs and networks.

8. _____ involve long-term efforts to cheat people out of their money.

9. The _____ _____ view is that some business organizations promote white-collar criminality.

10. According to the _____-_____ view, the motives that produce white-collar crimes are the same as those that produce any other criminal behaviors.

11. A major premise of the _____ _____ theory is that the Mafia is centrally coordinated by a national committee that settles disputes, dictates policy, and assigns territory.

12. One view of organized crime believes that there is a national syndicate of 25 or so Italian-dominated crime families that call themselves _____ _____ _____.

13. RICO stands for Racketeer Influenced and _____ Organiation.

14. An individual convicted under RICO is subject to _____ years in prison.

15. A number of reigning family heads are quite old, prompting some law enforcement officials to dub them "the _____ _____."

ESSAY QUESTIONS

1. What has caused the alleged erosion of Mafia power?

2. Discuss compliance strategies.

3. Discuss securities fraud; include churning, front running, and bucketing.

4. Differentiate between white-collar crime and organized crime.

5. Discuss the research concerning environmental crime.

CHAPTER 12 ANSWER SECTION

.MULTIPLE CHOICE

1. b
2. d
3. c
4. d
5. c
6. c
7. b
8. a
9. d
10. b
11. a
12. c
13. a
14. b
15. a
16. b
17. c
18. b
19. c
20. d

TRUE/FALSE

1. T
2. F
3. F
4. T
5. T
6. F
7. T
8. T
9. T
10. F
11. T
12. F
13. T
14. F
15. F

FILL-IN REVIEW

1. White-collar crime
2. corporate
3. Organized
4. Clean Water
5. Trojan horse
6. salami slice
7. virus
8. Stings, or swindles
9. corporate culture
10. self-control view
11. alien conspiracy theory
12. La Cosa Nostra
13. Corrupt
14. 20
15. Geritol gang

13 Public Order Crimes

LEARNING OBJECTIVES

After covering the material in this chapter, you should understand:

1. what a public order crime is, and be able to give examples.

2. why the legislation of moral issues has continually frustrated lawmakers.

3. Becker's concept of the moral entrepreneur.

4. the goals of moral crusades.

5. the relationship between homosexuality and the law.

6. the types of outlawed sexual behaviors defined as paraphilias.

7. the differences between the types of prostitutes.

8. the debates surrounding the legalization of prostitution.

9. what the research tells us about the relationship between pornography and violence.

10. the relationship between pornography and the law.

11. concern about drug abuse across the United States, its prohibition, and its extent.

12. the various views discussed about drug abuse.

13. the relationship between drug abuse and crime.

14. the various drug control strategies that are discussed.

15. the issues surrounding legalization, or decriminalization, of restricted drugs.

KEYWORDS

public order crime
victimless crime
moral entrepreneur
gay bashing
homosexuality
sodomy
homophobia
paraphilia
prostitution
streetwalker
brothel
madam
call girl
circuit traveler

pornography
obscenity
temperance movement
Prohibition
narcotic

CHAPTER OUTLINE

I. Law and morality
    1. legislation of moral issues has continually frustrated lawmakers
    2. "victimless crimes" (such as pornography, prostitution, etc.) erode the moral fabric of society and therefore should be prohibited and punished
    A. Criminal or immoral?
        1. acts that most of us deem highly immoral are not criminal
        2. some acts (such as euthanasia) that seem both well-intentioned and moral are nonetheless considered criminal
        3. immoral acts can be distinguished from crimes on the basis of social harm they cause
    B. Moral crusaders
        1. public order crimes often trace their origin to moral crusaders
        2. Howard Becker calls these people moral entrepreneurs, or rule creators
        3. moral crusades are often directed against people clearly defined as evil by one segment of the population, even though they may be admired by others

II. Homosexuality
    1. gay bashing
    2. homosexuality derives from the Greek *homos*, meaning "same"
    A. Attitudes toward homosexuality
        1. Bible implies that God destroyed the ancient cities of Sodom and Gomorrah because of their residents' deviant behavior, presumably homosexuality
        2. Bible expressly forbids homosexuality
        3. homophobia is an extreme overreaction to homosexuals
        4. constant reminders of antigay sentiments
    B. Homosexuality and the law
        1. homosexuality is no longer a crime in the U.S.
            a. in the case of *Robinson v. California*, the U.S. Supreme Court determined that people could not be criminally prosecuted because of their status
        2. illegal to deprive gay men and women of due process of law
        3. oral and anal sex and all other forms of intercourse that are not heterosexual and genital are banned in about half the U.S. states
        4. 1986, the Supreme Court, in *Bowers v. Hardwick*, upheld a Georgia statute making it a crime to engage in consensual sodomy
        5. about 25 states have adopted the American Law Institute's Model Penal Code policy of legalizing any private, consensual sexual behavior between adults; however, the remaining states still treat sodomy as a felony
        6. U.S. military bans openly gay people from serving but has comprised with a "don't ask, don't tell' policy
    C. Is the tide turning?
        1. increase in social tolerance
        2. November 1998, by a vote of 6-1, the Georgia Supreme Court struck down the state's 182-year-old sodomy law that was the basis for the *Bowers v. Hardwick* decision

III. Paraphilias
    1. paraphilias are bizarre or abnormal sexual practices involving recurrent sexual urges focused on:

          a. nonhuman objects
          b. humiliation or the experience of receiving or giving pain
          c. children or others who cannot grant consent
      2. paraphilia behavior includes: frotteurism, voyeurism, exhibitionism, sadomasochism, and pedophilia
      3. paraphilias can lead to sexual assault in which victims suffer severe harm.

IV.   Prostitution
      1. modern commercial sex appears to have its roots in ancient Greece, where Solon established licensed brothels in 500 B.C.
      2. prostitution can be defined as the granting of nonmarital sexual access, established by mutual agreement of the prostitutes, their clients, and their employers, for remuneration
      3. Prasad found that decisions to employ a prostitute are shaped by sexuality as well as by peer pressure, the wish for sexual exchange free from obligations, and curiosity
   A.   Incidence of prostitution
      1. difficult to assess the number of prostitutes operating in the U.S.
      2. UCR indicates that about 100,000 prostitution arrests are made annually
          a. gender ratio is 3:4 female
          b. about 1,000 arrests are of minors under the age of 18
      3. arguments that criminal law should not interfere with sexual transactions because no one is harmed are undermined by these disturbing statistics
   B.   Types of prostitutes
      1. streetwalkers
      2. bar girls (B-girls)
      3. brothel prostitutes
      4. call girls
      5. escort services
          a. call house is a relatively new phenomenon
      6. circuit travelers
   C.   Becoming a prostitute
      1. male and female prostitutes often come from troubled homes and from poor urban areas or rural communities
          a. many were initiated into sex by family members as young as 10 to 12 years
      2. research indicates that few girls are forced into prostitution by a pimp
      3. there is evidence that both male and females enter prostitution voluntarily
   D.   Legalize prostitution?
      1. feminists have conflicting views of prostitution
          a. sexual equality view
          b. free choice view
      2. both positions argue that the penalties for prostitution should be reduced
          a. neither side advocates outright legalization

V.   Pornography
      1. term pornography derives from the Greek, *porne*, meaning "prostitute," and *graphein,* meaning "to write"
      2. problem of controlling pornography centers on the definition of obscenity
          a. police /law enforcement officials can legally seize only material that is judged obscene
      3. because of legal and moral ambiguity, the sex trade is booming around the U.S.
   A.   Is pornography harmful?
      1. opponents of pornography argue that it degrades everyone
      2. one uncontested danger of pornography is "kiddie porn"
          a. each year more than a million children are believed to be used in pornography or prostitution, many of them runaways
      3. Ann Wolbert Burgess studied 55 child pornography rings:

        a.   solo

        b.   transition

        c.   syndicated

B.   Does pornography cause violence?

1. issue critical to the debate over pornography is whether viewing produces sexual or assaultive behavior
2. some evidence exists that viewing sexually explicit material actually has little effect on behavior
3. little or no documentation of a correlation between pornography and violent crime
4. there is strong evidence that people exposed to material that portrays violence, sadism, and women enjoying being raped and degraded are likely to be sexually aggressive toward women

C.   Pornography and the law

1. First Amendment of the U.S. Constitution protects free speech
2. cases of *Roth v. United States* and *Alberts v. California*, the U.S. Supreme Court declared that "...implicit in the history of the First Amendment is the rejection of obscenity as utterly without redeeming social importance"
   a. declaration did not clearly define obscenity
3. Supreme Court redefined its concept of obscenity in the case of *Miller v. California*
4. *Pope v. Illinois* articulated a reasonableness doctrine

D.   Controlling sex for profit

1. sex for profit predates Western civilization
2. a concerted effort by the federal government to prosecute adult movie distributors
3. alternative approach has been to restrict the sale of pornography within acceptable boundaries

E.   Technological Change

1. technological change will provide the greatest challenge to those seeking to control the sex-for-profit industry
2. the Communications Decency Act (CDA)
3. The Child Online Protection Act (H.R. 3783)

VI.   Substance abuse

1. problem of substance abuse stretches across the U.S.
2. increasing number of drug-related arrests
3. some view it as another type of victimless public order crime
4. great debate over the legalization of drugs and the control of alcohol

A.   When did drug use begin?

1. use of substances to change reality and provide stimulation, relief, or relaxation has gone on for thousands of years
2. drug use was accepted in Europe well into the twentieth century
3. in the early years of the U.S., opium and its derivatives were easily obtained
   a. by the turn of the twentieth century, an estimated 1 million U.S. citizens were opiate users

B.   Alcohol and its prohibition

1. history of alcohol and the law in the U.S. has been controversial and dramatic
2. the temperance movement
   a. ratification of the Eighteenth Amendment in 1919
3. Prohibition failed.
   a. 1933, the Twenty-First Amendment to the Constitution repealed Prohibition

C.   The extent of substance abuse

1. use of mood-altering substances persists in the U.S.
2. national surveys show that drug use is now less common than it was two decades ago
3. one important source of information on drug use is the annual self-report survey of high school youth
4. data indicate that the drug problem has not gone away and may be increasing among high school youth

D. The causes of substance abuse
1. the subcultural view
2. psychodynamic view
3. genetic basis
4. observing parental drug use
5. problem behavior syndrome (PBS)
6. rational choice view
7. there does not seem to be one single cause of substance abuse

E. Drugs and crime
1. significant association believed to exist between drug abuse and crime
2. important precipitating factor in domestic assault, armed robbery, and homicide cases
3. relationship remains uncertain
4. important source of data on the drug abuse-crime connection is the federally sponsored Arrestee Drug Abuse Monitoring Program (ADAM)

F. Drugs and the law
1. 1914, the Harrison Narcotic Act
2. 1970, the Comprehensive Drug Act
3. various federal laws have attempted to increase penalties
4. more than 30 jurisdictions have passed laws providing severe penalties for drunk drivers, including mandatory jail sentences

G. Drug control strategies
1. systematic apprehension of large-volume drug dealers
   a. enforcement of strict drug laws that carry heavy penalties
2. intercepting drug supplies as they enter the country
3. direct efforts at large-scale drug rings
4. prosecution and punishment of drug offenders a top priority
   a. average sentence for drug offenders sent to federal prison is about six years
5. involvement of local community groups
6. use the civil justice system to harass offenders
7. drug education and prevention strategies (such as DARE)
8. drug testing of private employees, government workers, and criminal offenders
9. long-term effect of treatment, on drugs, however, is still uncertain
10. research indicates that drug abusers who obtain and keep employment will end or reduce the incidence of their substance abuse

H. Legalization
1. commentators have called for the legalization or decriminalization of restricted drugs since the so-called war on drugs is expensive
2. Naadelmann opposed
3. if legalized, government could control price and distribution
4. legalization would increase the nation's rate of drug usage
5. decriminalization or legalization of controlled substances is unlikely in the near future

VI. Summary

MULTIPLE CHOICE

1. Public order crimes often trace their origin to _____ who seek to shape the law toward their own way of thinking.
    a. judges
    b. reformists
    c. moral crusaders
    d. socialists

2. Today's moral crusaders take on such issues as
    a. prayer in school.
    b. the right to legal abortion.
    c. the distribution of sexually explicit books.
    d. All of the above.

3. People who seek to control or criminalize deviant behaviors are called
    a. legislatures.
    b. moral entrepreneurs.
    c. police officers.
    d. power seekers.

4. Gays were brutalized and killed by the ancient
    a. Greeks.
    b. Romans.
    c. Hebrews.
    d. Egyptians.

5. Until the Revolution, some American colonies punished homosexuality with
    a. death.
    b. banishment.
    c. imprisonment.
    d. torture.

6. In 1998, voters in the state of _____ repealed a law protecting gays from discrimination.
    a. Vermont
    b. Rhode Island
    c. Connecticut
    d. Maine

7. Aside from _____, (which has civil unions) no state or locality allows any form of same-sex marriage.
    a. Vermont
    b. Rhode Island
    c. Connecticut
    d. Maine

8. What is the common sentence if one is convicted of having any form of intercourse that is not heterosexual and genital?
    a. three years
    b. five years
    c. eight years
    d. ten years

9. Paraphilias have existed and been recorded for thousands of years. _____ texts more than 2000 years old contain references to such sexually deviant behaviors.
    a. Egyptian
    b. Buddhist

c. Hindu

d. Greek

10. Deriving pleasure from receiving pain or inflicting pain on another is
   a. pedophilia.
   b. frotteurism.
   c. voyeurism.
   d. sadomasochism.

11. The earliest record of prostitution appears in ancient _____, where priests engaged is sex to promote fertility in the community.
   a. Egypt
   b. Mesopotamia
   c. Rome
   d. Greece

12. In ancient Greece, the earnings of prostitutes helped pay for the temple of
   a. Aphrodite.
   b. Medusa.
   c. Ionesius.
   d. Venus.

13. Which of the following conditions is not present in a commercial sexual transaction?
   a. activity that has sexual significance for the prostitute
   b. economic transaction
   c. emotional indifference
   d. All of the above.

14. Prior to the nineteenth century, pornography essentially involved the
   a. photographic image.
   b. use of males only.
   c. written word.
   d. work of artists.

15.   Each year more than _____ children are believed to be used in pornography or prostitution.
   a. 10,000
   b. 100,000
   c. 1,000,000
   d. 10,000,000

16. Which serial killer claimed his murderous rampage was fueled by reading pornography?
   a. Ted Bundy
   b. Richard Speck
   c. Jack the Ripper
   d. the Green River Stalker

17. In Canada, _____ and _____ are considered serious urban problems.
   a. cocaine, heroin
   b. heroin, methamphetamine
   c. marijuana, crack
   d. crack, cocaine

18. At the turn of the century, _____ was viewed as a threat to the lifestyle of the majority of the nation's population, then living on farms and in villages.
   a. immigration
   b. urbanism

    c. Catholicism
    d. socialism

19. At the time of the Crusades, the _____ were using marijuana.
    a. English
    b. Spanish
    c. Arabs
    d. Jews

20. Prohibition was enforced by the _____ Act.
    a. Volstead
    b. Temperance
    c. Harrison Narcotics
    d. Ness

TRUE/FALSE

1. The sub-cultural view views drug abuse as having an environmental basis.

2. Substance abuse is an ancient practice dating back more than 4,000 years.

3. There does not seem to be a strong link between drug abuse and crime.

4. Drug use in general has stabilized in the U.S.

5. The source control approach directs efforts to severely punish known drug dealers and traffickers.

6. DARE is based on the concept that young students need specific analytical social skills to resist peer pressure and refuse drugs.

7. The Maine Supreme Court struck the state's 182-year-old sodomy law that was the basis for the *Bowers v. Hardwick* decision in 1998.

8. Frotteurism is the rubbing against or touching a nonconsenting person in a crowd, elevator, or other public place.

9. Brothel prostitutes are the aristocrats of prostitution.

10. There is a great deal of documentation demonstrating that a correlation exists between pornography and violent crime.

11. The Fifth Amendment of the U.S. Constitution protects free speech and prohibits police agencies from liming the public's right of free expression.

12. Although being a homosexual is not a crime, it is illegal to engage in homosexual acts in about half the U.S. states.

13. The Supreme Court has ruled obscenity "is in the eyes of the beholder."

14. Some experts suggest that substance abuse may have a genetic basis.

15. Substance abuse appears to be an important precipitating factor in domestic assault, armed robbery, and homicide cases.

FILL-IN REVIEW

1. Legislation of _____ issues has continually frustrated lawmakers.

2. Howard Becker refers to rule creators as _____ _____.

3. The line between behavior that are merely _____ and those that are _____ is often blurred.

4. _____ _____ has been coined to describe violent acts directed at people because of their sexual orientation.

5. An extremely negative overreaction to homosexuals is referred to as _____.

6. _____ is obtaining sexual pleasure from spying on a stranger while he or she disrobes or engages in sexual behavior with another.

7. The UCR indicates that about _____ prostitution arrests are made annually.

8. Of all the prostitutes, _____ have the highest incidence of drug abuse.

9. The aristocrats of prostitution are _____ _____.

10. Prostitutes known as _____ _____ move around in groups of two or three to lumber, labor, and agricultural camps.

11. Research indicates that few girls are forced into prostitution by a _____.

12. One uncontested danger of pornography is "_____ porn."

13. To control the spread of _____ pornography, Congress passed the CDA.

14. _____ are deviant sexual acts such as exhibitionism and voyeurism.

15. The Supreme Court has ruled that material is _____ if it has prurient sexual content and is devoid of social value.

ESSAY QUESTIONS

1. Legislation of moral issues has continually frustrated lawmakers. Explain why.

2. What does the research tell us about men who hire prostitutes? About the incidence of prostitution?

3. Does pornography cause violence? What does the research tell us?

4. Select two of the views on the cause of drug use, and discuss them.

5. Discuss two of the drug control strategies discussed in your text. Which one do you think will be most effective? Why?

CHAPTER 13 ANSWER SECTION

MULTIPLE CHOICE

1.	c
2.	d
3.	b
4.	c
5.	a
6.	d
7.	a
8.	d
9.	b
10.	d
11.	b
12.	a
13.	a
14.	c
15.	c
16.	a
17.	d
18.	b
19.	c
20.	a

TRUE/FALSE

1.	T
2.	T
3.	F
4.	T
5.	F
6.	T
7.	F
8.	T
9.	F
10.	F
11.	F
12.	T
13.	F
14.	T
15.	T

FILL-IN REVIEW

1.	moral
2.	moral entrepreneurs
3.	immoral, criminal
4.	Gay bashing
5.	homophobia
6.	Voyeurism
7.	100,000
8.	streetwalkers
9.	call girls
10.	circuit travelers
11.	pimp
12.	kiddie
13.	Internet
14.	Paraphilias
15.	obscene

14 The Criminal Justice System

LEARNING OBJECTIVES

After covering the material in this chapter, you should understand:

1. the concept of the criminal justice system.

2. the role of police and law enforcement in the criminal justice system.

3. the criminal court system, and the court structure.

4. the differences between the roles played by the prosecution and the defense.

5. the following correctional sanctions: probation, incarceration, jail, prison, and parole.

6. the decision points involved in the processing of a felony offender.

7. why the criminal justice system can be compared to a funnel.

8. the law of criminal procedure.

9. the differences between the following concepts of criminal justice; crime control model, justice model, due process model, rehabilitation model, nonintervention model, and the restorative justice model.

KEYWORDS

criminal justice system
discretion
landmark decision
adversary system
prosecutor
defendant
defense attorney
right to counsel
public defender
pro bono
probation
incarceration
jail
prison
penitentiary
parole
arrest
probable cause
booking
interrogation
indictment
grand jury
preliminary hearing
arraignment
bail

recognizance
plea bargain
hung jury
disposition
appeal
courtroom work group
law of criminal procedure
Bill of Rights
crime control model
Miranda rights
exclusionary rule
justice model
determinate sentencing
due process model
rehabilitation model
noninterventionist model
restorative justice model

CHAPTER OUTLINE

I.   The concept of a criminal justice system
     1. criminal justice agencies have existed for only 150 years or so
     2. modern era of criminal justice began with a series of explorations of the criminal justice process
     3. 1967, Lyndon administration published *The Challenge of Crime in a Free Society*
         a. Safe Streets and Crime Control Act of 1968

II. What is the criminal justice system?
     1. agencies of government charged with enforcing law, adjudicating crime, and correcting criminal conduct; an instrument of social control
     2. employs close to 2 million people
     3. major components: police, the courts, and correctional agencies
     A. Police and law enforcement
         1. approximately 17,000 law enforcement agencies operate in the U.S.
         2. police are the most visible agents of the justice process
         3. police discretion has been of some concern, as has corruption
         4. police departments have experimented with new forms of law enforcement
     B. The criminal court system
         1. criminal courts are the core elements in the administration of criminal justice
         2. court is a complex social agency
         3. U.S. criminal justice can be selective in that discretion accompanies defendants through every step of the process
         4. typical state court structure is multitiered: lower courts, superior trial courts, appellate courts
         5. federal court system has three tiers: U.S. district courts, intermediate appellate courts, U.S. Supreme Court
         6. rulings by the U.S. Supreme Court are usually referred to as landmark decisions
         7. the prosecutor and the defense attorney are opponents in an adversary system
         8. any person accused of a crime has the right to counsel
     C. Corrections
         1. most common correctional treatment is probation
         2. jails hold those convicted of misdemeanors and those awaiting trial or involved in other proceedings, such as grand jury deliberations
         3. state and federally operated facilities that receive felony offenders sentenced by the criminal courts are called prisons or penitentiaries

4. parole is a process whereby an inmate is selected for early release and serves the remainder of the sentence in the community under the supervision of a parole officer

III. The process of justice
   1. initial contact
   2. investigation
   3. arrest
   4. custody
   5. complaint
   6. grand jury (preliminary hearing)
   7. arraignment
   8. bail
   9. plea bargain
   10. adjudication
   11. disposition
   12. postconviction remedy
   13. correctional treatment
   14. release
   15. aftercare
   16. criminal justice system can be compared to a funnel
   17. trials are rare

IV. Criminal justice and the rule of law
   1. criminal procedure sets out and guarantees citizens certain rights and privileges when they are accused of crime
   2. procedural laws control the actions of the agencies of justice and define the rights of criminal defendants
   3. Bill of Rights is most important source of law

V. Concepts of justice
   A. Crime control model
      1. overriding purpose of the criminal justice system is to protect the public, deter criminal behavior, and incapacitate known criminals
      2. proponents lobby for abolition of the exclusionary rule
      3. emphasizes protecting society and compensating victims
      4. has become a dominant force in American justice
   B. Justice model
      1. futile to rehabilitate criminals
      2. advocates question the crime control perspective's reliance on deterrence
      3. calls for fairness in criminal processes and determinate sentencing
      4. has had an important influence on criminal justice policy
   C. Due process model
      1. combines the elements of liberal/positivist criminology with the legal concept of procedural fairness for the accused
      2. due process principles call for individualized justice, treatment, and rehabilitation of offenders
      3. demands that defense counsel, jury trials, and other procedural safeguards be offered to every criminal defendant
      4. seen as protector of civil rights
      5. justice system remains an adversary process
      6. orientation has not fared well in recent years
   D. Rehabilitation model
      1. embraces the notion that given the proper care and treatment, criminals can be changed into productive, law-abiding citizens
      2. a method for dispensing "treatment" to needy "patients"
   E. Nonintervention model

127

1. calls for limiting government intrusion into the lives of people
2. pushes for deinstitutionaliziation of nonserious offenders, and decriminalization of nonserious offenses
3. skeptical about the creation of laws that criminalize acts that were previously legal
4. criticism of this philosophy is that there is little evidence that alternative programs actually result in "widening the net"
    F. Restorative justice model
1. draws its inspiration from religious and philosophical teachings
2. claims that the state efforts to punish and control encourage crime
3. guided by three essential principles: community "ownership" of conflict; material and symbolic reparation for crime victims; and social reintegration of the offender
4. has become an important perspective in recent years, but questions are now being raised about its effectiveness
    G. Concepts of justice today
1. emphasis on protecting the public by increasing criminal sentences and swelling prison populations
2. the door to treatment for nonviolent, nonchronic offenders has not been closed

VI. Summary

MUTLIPLE CHOICE

1. Criminal justice refers to agencies of government charged with enforcing law, adjudicating crime, and
    a. making laws.
    b. hiring police officers.
    c. correcting criminal conduct.
    d. All of the above.

2. Your text tells us that it costs about _____ per year to keep juveniles in an institution.
    a. $25,000
    b. $30,000
    c. $50,000
    d. $70,000

3. About how many million people are arrested for serious felony offenses each year?
    a. 2
    b. 3
    c. 4
    d. 5

4. _____ are the most visible agents of the justice process.
    a. Judges
    b. Prosecutors
    c. Defense attorneys
    d. Police

5. Which courts conduct the preliminary processing of felony offenses?
    a. lower courts
    b. superior trial courts
    c. appellate courts
    d. superior appellate courts

6. Which courts have jurisdiction over cases involving violations of federal law?
    a. the U.S. Supreme Court
    b. U.S. district courts
    c. intermediate federal courts of appeal
    d. state Supreme Courts

7. The _____ is responsible for bringing the case to trial and to a final conclusion.
    a. judge
    b. defense attorney
    c. prosecutor
    d. grand jury

8. The _____ participates in bail hearings, presents cases before a grand jury, and appears for the state at arraignments.
    a. judge
    b. defense attorney
    c. prosecutor
    d. grand jury

9. The prosecutor, like the _____, exercises a great deal of discretion.
    a. judge
    b. police
    c. grand jury
    d. defense attorney

10. The federal court system has long provided counsel to the indigent on the basis of the _____ Amendment of the U.S. Constitution.
     a. First
     b. Fourth
     c. Fifth
     d. Sixth

11. If a defense lawyer volunteers his/her services, the lawyer is working
     a. per bonus.
     b. pro bono.
     c. con bono.
     d. per con.

12. _____ is a legal disposition that allows the convicted offender to remain in the community, subject to conditions imposed by court order under the supervision of a probation officer.
     a. Parole
     b. Incarceration
     c. Probation
     d. Electronic supervision

13. Procedural laws have several different sources. Most important are the first _____ amendments to the U.S. Constitution.
     a. 3
     b. 5
     c. 7
     d. 10

14. Advocates of the crime control model lobby for abolition of
     a. due process.
     b. Miranda rights.
     c. the exclusionary rule.
     d. capital punishment.

15. The _____ philosophy emphasizes protecting society and compensating victims.
     a. crime control model
     b. justice model
     c. due process model
     d. rehabilitation model

16. The _____ view of the justice system portrays it as a method for dispensing "treatment" to needy "patients."
     a. crime control model
     b. justice model
     c. due process model
     d. rehabilitation model

17. This model advocates deinstitutionalization of nonserious offenders.
     a. crime control model
     b. nonintervention model
     c. due process model
     d. restorative justice model

18. This model believes that that the true purpose of the criminal justice system is to promote a peaceful, just society.
     a. crime control model

b. nonintervention model
c. due process model
d. restorative justice model

19. Advocates of the _____ model question the crime control perspective's reliance on deterrence.
    a. justice
    b. nonintervention
    c. due process
    d. restorative justice

20. The crime control model is rooted in which theory?
    a. social structure
    b. choice
    c. social process
    d. social control

TRUE/FALSE

1. It costs about $70,000 to build a prison cell.

2. Every state except Alaska maintains a state police force.

3. About 15 million people are being arrested each year.

4. Attorneys are the most visible agents of the justice process.

5. The criminal courts are considered by many to be the core element in the administration of criminal justice.

6. The U.S. Supreme Court is the highest federal district court.

7. The U.S. Supreme Court is composed of nine members.

8. Within the structure of the court system, the prosecutor and the defense attorney are opponents in what is known as the adversary system.

9. The federal court system has only recently provided counsel to the indigent on the basis of the Sixth Amendment of the U.S. Constitution.

10. The most common correctional treatment is parole.

11. In about half the states and in the federal system, the decision of whether to bring a suspect to trial is made by a group of citizens brought together to form a preliminary jury.

12. Another name for the preliminary hearing is the probable cause hearing.

13. Sentencing an offender to death is a form of disposition.

14. Prison sentences imposed by state courts are becoming shorter on the average.

15. The first 10 Amendments of the U.S. Constitution are generally called the Declaration of Independence.

FILL-IN REVIEW

1. An _____ occurs when the police take a person into custody for allegedly committing a criminal act.

2. An _____ brings the accused before the court that will actually try the case.

3. The criminal justice system can be compared to a _____.

4. Today, ìach component of the justice system is closely supervised by state and federal courts through the law of _____ _____.

5. The _____ _____ model believe that the overriding purpose of the justice system is to protect the public, deter criminal behavior, and incapacitate known criminals.

6. According to the _____ model, it is futile to rehabilitate criminals.

7. Advocates of the _____ _____ model see themselves as protectors of civil rights.

8. The _____ model embraces the notion that given the proper care and treatment, criminals can be changed into productive law-abiding citizens.

9. The _____ model calls for limiting government intrusion into the lives of people, especially minors, who run afoul of the law.

10. The _____ _____ model draws its inspiration from religious and philosophical teachings.

11. The first 10 amendments to the U.S. Constitution are generally called the _____ _____ _____.

12. Many jurisdictions allow defendants awaiting trial to be released on their own _____.

13. The decision of whether to bring a suspect to trial is referred to as an _____.

14. The purpose of _____ is to help the ex-inmate bridge the gap between institutional confinement and a positive adjustment within the community.

15. _____ _____ refers to the agencies of government charged with enforcing law, adjudicating crime, and correcting criminal conduct.

ESSAY QUESTIONS

1. Compare and contrast the justice model with the restorative justice model of crime.

2. Discuss problems surrounding the tremendous discretion afforded police officers.

3. Discuss the role of the U.S. Supreme Court.

4. Discuss the two major functions of the defense attorney.

5. Discuss why the criminal justice system is compared to a funnel.

CHAPTER 14 ANSWER SECTION

MULTIPLE CHOICE		TRUE/FALSE	
1.	c	1.	T
2.	b	2.	F
3.	b	3.	T
4.	d	4.	F
5.	a	5.	T
6.	b	6.	F
7.	c	7.	T
8.	c	8.	T
9.	b	9.	F
10.	d	10.	F
11.	b	11.	F
12.	c	12.	T
13.	d	13.	T
14.	c	14.	T
15.	a	15.	F
16.	d		
17.	b		
18.	d		
19.	a		
20.	b		

FILL-IN REVIEW

1. arrest
2. arraignment
3. funnel
4. criminal procedure
5. crime control
6. justice model
7. due process
8. rehabilitation
9. interventionist
10. restorative justice
11. Bill of Rights
12. recognizance
13. indictment
14. parole
15. criminal justice